WRITING MUSIC FOR HIT SONGS

WRITING MUSIC FOR HIT SONGS

Including New Songs from the '90s

Jai Josefs

Schirmer Books
An Imprint of Simon & Schuster Macmillan
New York

Prentice Hall International
London   Mexico City   New Delhi   Singapore   Sydney   Toronto

Copyright © 1989, 1996 by Jai Josefs

The permissions for the music examples in this book appear on pages 241–251.

Schirmer Books
An Imprint of Simon & Schuster Macmillan
1633 Broadway
New York, NY 10019

Library of Congress Catalog Card Number: 96–10359

Printed in the United States of America

Printing number

2   3   4   5   6   7   8   9   10

Library of Congress Cataloging-in-Publication Data:
Josefs, Jai, 1947–
    Writing Music for hit songs : including new songs from the '90s / Jai Josefs.
        p.   cm.
    Includes indexes.
    ISBN 0–02–864678–9 (alk. paper)
    1. Popular music—Writing and publishing.   2. Popular music—Instruction and study.   3. Music—Theory.   I. Title.
MT67.J79   1996
782.42164'13—dc20   96–10359
                                                                                      CIP
                                                                                      MN

The paper used in this publication meets the requirements of ANSI/NISO Z39.48-1992 (Permanence of Paper).

Contents

v

Introduction

In 1977, when the late Helen King asked if I would be willing to teach a music-writing class at Songwriters' Resources and Services in Los Angeles (later to become the National Academy of Songwriters), I had recently arrived from Boston and was working primarily as a musician and arranger/producer. After starting to teach classes at SRS, however, I noticed that the aspects of theory relevant to the needs of up-and-coming songwriters were somewhat different from those I had studied and taught at music schools back east.

As I gradually began to evolve my program to meet those needs, I became aware of another interesting fact: *There was no book on music theory and composition that was specifically directed toward songwriters and those involved in contemporary popular music.* In fact, most theory books use classical music to illustrate the topics that are presented, except for the few that draw primarily from jazz. And while I would never diminish the importance of my jazz or classical training, I think understanding how Elton John, Babyface, and Alan Jackson develop their melodies is much more relevant to writing a hit song than analyzing how Bach or Duke Ellington did. Furthermore, though there are several excellent books for songwriters on the market, most of them deal primarily with lyrics and/or the business aspects of a songwriting career, and the few that do touch on music devote at best only one chapter to some of the bare essentials.

As I began both to focus my own career on songwriting and to teach songwriting seminars around the country, more and more people began to ask me if I knew of a book they could work with at home that would address their specific needs in writing and performing contemporary popular music. Slowly and inevitably I realized that someone would eventually have to write one. Ideally, that person would be a working songwriter, arranger, and musician who had been formally trained in both classical and jazz and who had experience in a variety of current styles including pop, country, R&B, and rock and roll as well as the ability to teach and communicate effectively. After an exhaustive survey, I couldn't find anyone else with the appropriate qualifications who was willing to take a year and a half out of his or her life to write it, so I figured I might as well do it myself.

Seriously though, *Writing Music for Hit Songs* was created with the intention of providing you, the songwriter or writer/performer, with a comprehensive guide through the maze of elements involved in musically crafting a successful popular song. There is truly nothing in this book that you couldn't figure out for yourself after two or three years of education in a good music school and several hundred hours of listening to, transcribing, and analyzing hit tunes. What I have done is to organize and simplify the process so you can learn what is relevant to *your* needs in a simple, concise, step-by-step fashion and spend the rest of the time applying it to writing your *own* hits.

One final point needs to be addressed before I send you out on that journey. The question I'm most frequently asked in my seminars and workshops is, "Do the writers whose songs you analyze actually know and apply all this theoretical information? Don't they just write what they feel and have it come out great?" In other words, is it worth your while to undertake even this pared-down-to-the-essentials study of theory and composition?

Several years ago a friend of mine, knowing that I was going to be vacationing on the Oregon coast, invited me to spend some time with her and her friends John Smith and Valerie Day of the hit group Nu Schooz ("I Can't Wait," "Point of No Return"), who were ensconced in a cabin in the area writing material for their next album. After dinner, a couple of beers, and some jamming on guitar and synthesizers, John, who seemed to be a typical, young, long-haired, "write-what-you-feel" type, called me over and said, "Hey, you teach songwriting, take a look at this." He proceeded to show me a book in which he had musically analyzed every song Stevie Wonder had recorded for verse/chorus structure, key changes, rhythmic groove, chord progressions, etc. While not every successful music writer has conducted such an extensive study, the truth is that virtually all of them have "paid their dues" through years of playing, studying, and analyzing the hits of the past. What this book offers is a structured, guided tour through the best pop, rock, country, R&B, film, and theater songs of our generation so you can learn what it *took* to write music for the most successful songs of yesterday. Hopefully, with hard work and a positive attitude, you'll have a fighting chance at seeing if you have what it takes to write the hits of tomorrow. Good luck!

How to Use This Book

Learning music from the printed page presents a unique problem. Music is sound in action, and intellectually understanding how to use a particular melody or chord progression does not necessarily mean you can successfully integrate it into your writing. When I make a point in a class or seminar I'm teaching, I always go directly to the keyboard and illustrate it so that the participants can actually *hear* what I'm talking about.

Throughout this book you will find more than 150 musical examples which I intended to be used in exactly that manner. I strongly encourage you to put down the text for a moment and actually play and/or sing each one of them when it appears, so you develop an aural as well as a theoretical comprehension of the material I'm presenting. Those of you who already read music will have little difficulty in doing this. We originally intended to release a cassette of those examples along with the book for those of you who do not, but technical copyright restrictions prevented us from doing so. If you're in that category, you can either have a friend who reads perform them for you, or listen to (or recall) the original recorded versions of the hit songs quoted, most of which will be quite familiar. It might even be a good time to begin learning to read and write music yourself, and if you choose to do so the material presented in Part Two (Chapters 4–6) will get you off to a good start.

A few words about the examples I selected. They have deliberately been drawn from the most widely heard songs of the last four decades in a variety of idioms recorded by artists ranging from the Beatles and Jimi Hendrix to Boyz II Men and Garth Brooks. This was done so that whether you write country and western or rhythm and blues, adult contemporary or hard rock and roll, you will get an insight into how some of your favorite tunes have been put together. I also tried to keep a healthy balance between "standards" from the '60s, '70s, '80s, and more current charted hits (as of 1996, when the current edition of the book was completed). One final note: When I encountered a discrepancy between the printed sheet music and the recorded version of a song (as was often the case), I generally chose to go with whatever combination of the two most simply and clearly illustrated the topic I was discussing.

At various points throughout the book you will find that I have included specific *exercises*. Again, I strongly urge you to put aside the text for a moment and take the time to write them out to make certain you fully understand each subject before going on to the next. The answers to most of these have been printed in an appendix in the back of the book, so you'll know whether you completed them accurately. I further suggest that you actually *play* those exercises to make sure that you hear as well as comprehend them. If you are not fluent on an instrument, you can either have a friend perform them for you or purchase a small, inexpensive electronic keyboard (many are available for less than $100), and use the material presented in Part Two to help you work them out yourself. The same advice holds true for those of you who are primarily vocalists or play only non-chordal instruments (such as the bass or saxophone) when dealing with exercises that involve chord progressions. I have also included a number of *assignments* where I request that you incorporate what we've discussed into writing an original song. You can do these either as you proceed or later on, at your discretion.

Above all, remember that Rome wasn't built in a day, and neither is a hit song. The material presented here is a distillation of years of music theory classes and information gathered from analyzing hundreds and hundreds of examples of the best of contemporary music. As Donovan said in a song from the *Brother Sun Sister Moon* soundtrack, "If you want your dreams to be . . . take your time, go slowly." This book was not meant to be digested in one or two (or even ten or twenty) sittings. If you're willing to proceed step-by-step, listen to each example, and complete each exercise as you go, I promise you'll have a breakthrough in your music that will have a permanent impact on everything you write. Enjoy!

Acknowledgements (First Edition)

When I agreed to write this book, I had no idea how involved and time consuming the process would be. Fortunately, I was able to draw upon the support of a wide variety of people without whose contributions the task would have either been impossible or driven me crazy.

First and foremost I need to acknowledge my "assistant" (for want of a better word) Madeleine Smith. If this book was my baby, then she truly was the midwife. From inputting all my rough drafts on computer (and actually making sense of them) to transcribing interviews with industry pros, to doing research on the hundreds of songs cited, to constantly providing me with feedback on every aspect of the text, her help was invaluable, to say the least, and I am deeply grateful.

Second, I want to thank all my past and present students, without whose constant questions and desire to learn I would never have evolved my system of teaching to the point where I could undertake a project like this. Particular appreciation goes out to Tanya Robinson, Dale Wells, and Phil Goldberg, who assisted me in many ways, not the least of which was serving as "guinea pigs" for several sections developed specifically for this book.

Special gratitude also goes out to my good friends and co-writers Alan O'Day and Harold Payne, who took the time to read my manuscript when I had completed the first draft and whose suggestions helped make the final version more readable. Thanks also to the music industry professionals, including songwriters Tom Snow, Diane Warren, Jay Graydon, Preston Glass, Michael Omartian, and Martin Page, publisher Carla Berkowitz, and producer Bob Margouleff, who took the time to share their insights with me so I could pass them along to you.

My editor, Julie Whaley, deserves special mention as well. She has consistently been a true partner in the project, for which I am most appreciative. Thanks also to Beth Franks for her incisive editorial input, and to my attorney, Stan Levy, who handled all my negotiations and whose friendship and support have been invaluable to me throughout my career.

Because writing this book nearly drove me crazy, I also need to acknowledge my friends and family who supported me through the process and helped keep me relatively sane, and my faithful cat Corwin, who spent hundreds of hours peacefully purring at my feet while I agonized over every chapter.

I am also indebted to a wide range of people who contributed in various ways including the staff at the National Academy of Songwriters, Dexter Moore and all the folks at BMI, Victor Cardell at the UCLA Archive of Popular American Music, music historian Brian Freeman, and vocalist Shelby Daniel.

Last but not least I want to acknowledge you, the reader, for taking the time and effort to invest in and work through this book. Thank you for letting me make a difference in helping you perfect your craft so that what you have to share as a songwriter can someday have an impact on all of us.

Preface to the Second Edition

The French have a saying, "Plus ça change, plus c'est la même chose," which roughly translated means "the more things change, the more they remain the same." As I look back on the years since the first edition of this book was published, those words definitely apply to popular music.

In 1987, Garth Brooks, Mariah Carey, and Boyz II Men were virtually unknown, Whitney Houston was an emerging new artist, and Lionel Richie and Kenny Rogers were major record sellers. Yet the basic principles of melody and chord progression then and now remain unchanged, and songwriters like Diane Warren, Tom Snow, and Michael Omartian, who are schooled in those principles, continue to turn out hits decade after decade.

When Schirmer Books offered me the opportunity to release an updated edition of *Writing Music For Hit Songs*, I was pleased at the chance to demonstrate that the information I wrote about in the first edition was still being used in the most current charted hits. As a result, although the basic structure of this book remains the same, over half of the music examples have been replaced by more contemporary hits that use the same techniques.

However, one difference between the musical worlds of the '80s and the present demanded special consideration. An innovative rhythm known as "new jack swing" has become the dominant groove in R&B, rap, and dance music, and has begun to infiltrate the pop charts as well. In response to this, I have added a completely new section to Chapter 19 analyzing the various aspects of this groove in detail.

Along with the rise of "new jack swing," there has been an increasing saturation of both the R&B and pop charts by groove-dominated rap and dance material. As a result, much of today's well-crafted songwriting has, in the words of the Bob McDill song, "Gone

Country." Because of this shift, I have included a substantially larger percentage of Nashville-based tunes as examples illustrating the songwriting principles I discuss. I have also added insights shared with me by successful country songwriters Randy Sharp and Angela Kaset and Nashville publisher Jody Williams, and I thank them for their participation.

I would also like to acknowledge three people without whom there would be no new edition: my editor Richard Carlin, who afforded me the opportunity to create it and impressed me with his ability to provide significant musical input as well; my agent Ronny Schiff, who guided me through the maze of technical and legal details involved in putting it together and spent many above-and-beyond-the-call-of-duty hours helping secure print rights for the musical examples; and my assistant and typist Joanna Bloem, who worked with me in the trenches and was a constant source of both good feedback and good humor.

I would further like to thank all my friends, family, and co-writers for being extremely patient with the disruptions in my schedule caused by the amount of time I had to put into this work. Very special thanks go out to Christy Shelton for the incredible amount of support she provided in so many ways throughout the entire process, and my faithful cat Corwin, who at the ripe old age of 14, continued to peacefully purr at my feet while I continued to agonize over every word. I also want to thank Eileen Haller for filling in when Joanna was unavailable, and my good friend Barry Kolsky for sharing his insights into the demo-making process.

Last but not least, I want to acknowledge all my students both past and present who, through their provocative questions and varied interests, make certain that my musical frame of reference continues to expand. Particular appreciation goes out to Dean Daley for sharing his extensive collection of contemporary country music and to Phil Goldberg (yes, the same Phil Goldberg from the first edition) for his generous research into the *Billboard* charts.

One of my greatest inspirations over the last decade has been seeing many of these students generate publishing, production, and even record deals by applying the techniques and principles outlined in this book. While knowledge of this material is by no means a guarantee of such success, it will certainly ensure that your songs will be competitive, your craft will be respected, and you will be able to adapt to the changing trends and styles of the industry. The rest is up to your own talent, vision, and determination. Good luck!

PART ONE

Laying the Groundwork

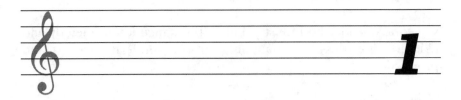

Beyond Melody

Many years ago I was introduced to a well-known producer with several platinum albums on his wall. Informed that I was a songwriter, he casually asked, "Oh, do you write lyrics or melodies?" While a person of his stature was obviously aware of all the musical components of a hit song, the fact that he grouped them under the category of "melody" points out a common misconception held by both beginning writers and people outside the music industry. In actuality, the musical component of contemporary hit songs consists of three distinct and equally important elements: *melody, rhythm,* and *harmony.*

Each of these elements plays a greater or lesser role depending on the style of music. For example, a collaborator of mine was once called in to an R&B/dance session by the producer to "help tie up loose ends and add some finishing touches." When she arrived at the session she was informed that the tracking (recording) of instruments was complete and the "finishing touches" required from her were the melody and lyrics for the singer! This may seem bizarre to

3

someone outside the industry, but in the dance idiom melody and lyric are often less important than groove (underlying beat) and production.

Rhythm

The effect of rhythm on a song becomes clear when you listen to the original Beatles' versions of "Got to Get You into My Life," "Fool on the Hill," and "With A Little Help from My Friends," and compare them to the remakes by Earth, Wind & Fire, Sergio Mendes, and Joe Cocker. Even though the melody and harmony are virtually unchanged, the new versions feel quite different because the basic rhythmic concept has been altered. Two recent examples of this occurred in 1987 when Club Nouveau took the old Bill Withers standard "Lean on Me" to number 1 on the *Billboard* charts, and in 1994 when vocalist Quino and his band Big Mountain scored a hit with Peter Frampton's "Baby I Love Your Way" by rerecording them with contemporary reggae grooves. While rhythm most dramatically affects dance material, its impact on any type of popular music, from easy country to hard rock and roll, should not be underestimated. In Chapter 19 we will explore in detail the specific components that make up the grooves used in these and other contemporary idioms.

Harmony

As songwriters, we must also be aware of the contribution of harmony (chord progression) to the overall musical effect of a song, especially in the case of ballads and so-called adult contemporary tunes where rhythm often plays a lesser role. Let's examine the first four measures of the melody of a well-known song by the late Brazilian composer Antonio Carlos Jobim (writer of such standards as "Girl from Ipanema" and "Quiet Nights"). Play or sing this melody before you continue, so you can relate our discussion of it to what you hear.

This is, to say the least, not a very involved melody in terms of range, although its melodic rhythm (placement of notes in time) holds some interest. (See Chapters 13 and 14 for a more detailed discussion of these terms.) Yet when Jobim harmonized it as follows, it became the "One Note Samba" that has been continuously performed and recorded throughout the world.

As you play the melody with the added harmony, notice how much richer and more interesting it sounds than in the unaccompanied version.

The concept of harmony is unique to Western music, i.e., that of Europe and America. Other systems of music (traditional Indian, Chinese, Japanese, African, etc.) do not have harmony. Instead, they have far more intricate melodies built on true or "just" scales, where all notes are acoustically related to the fundamental pitch. In the West, we use "tempered" scales in which notes are exactly equidistant from each other, altering the "natural" relationship so that an E played against an E chord is exactly the same as an E played against a C chord. This makes it possible for us to generate more complex harmony and modulate from key to key (see Chapters 7–11 for a more thorough explanation). Bach's famous "Well-Tempered Clavier," which explored the harmonic possibilities of the piano playing in every major and minor key, was a forerunner of today's harmonic techniques that have led us to the "One Note Samba" and beyond.

This musical heritage so pervades our listening that it is virtually impossible to hear the melody of a familiar pop song without also "hearing" the harmony. For example, play or sing this melody from Billy Joel's hit, "The Longest Time."

If you are familiar with the song, you will actually hear the first four bars and the second four bars slightly differently *even though the*

melody of each is exactly the same. That's because the harmony is different. (In Chapter 9 we'll discuss exactly what that difference is.)

Now listen to the melody again, this time with its chordal accompaniment.

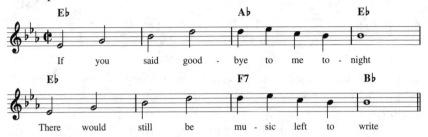

Finally, play or sing it a third time without harmonic accompaniment and notice how different each four-bar section sounds. That's because once we have listened to a song, *we only hear melody as colored by its harmony.*

Wrap-Up

In this book we'll be examining all three components of the music of today's (and tomorrow's) hits: harmony, melody, and rhythm. As a part of this investigation, we'll be analyzing excerpts from songs in a wide variety of contemporary idioms including pop, rock and roll, R&B, country, dance, film, and theater. If you're not familiar with any of the examples I have chosen, I strongly recommend listening to as many of the original recorded versions as possible. They have all reached millions of people, and as songwriters it is as important for us as it is for an auto mechanic or a brain surgeon to build on the successful techniques of those who have preceded us. As I stress constantly in my classes, we can be much more effective and innovative when we've mastered these techniques before attempting to add our own contributions.

Diane Warren, who has written over forty top ten hits for artists such as Michael Bolton, Celine Dion, Ace of Base, and Gloria Estefan, puts it like this: "The best way to develop as a writer is to listen to the really good songs, not the here-today-gone-tomorrow hits, and see exactly *why* they work. Then you can use them to inspire your own writing." That's exactly what you'll be doing as you continue through this book: examining the underlying principles of harmony, melody, and rhythm that form the basis of contemporary hit songs, analyzing excerpts from those songs so you can understand and hear how the principles apply, and doing specific exercises and writing assignments so you can integrate what you have learned into your own compositions. Many of my students have obtained publishing deals and even recordings through this course of study. It is my hope that your willingness to do the work involved will pay off with similar results.

2

Contemporary Song Forms and Hooks

Before we dive into the theory of how melody, harmony, and rhythm interact to create the musical part of a song, we first need to examine song form and structure. Just as classical composers had their sonatas and concertos containing specific sections following each other in prescribed ways, so today's contemporary pop composers use particular song forms as vehicles for the music *they* write. While there is no "formula" for a hit song, the fact that 99 percent of the music played on pop, rock, country, and R&B radio today is based on some variation of these forms makes them well worth a thorough examination.

Verse, Chorus, and Bridge: Building Blocks of Song Structure

Virtually all of the hit songs on the charts over the last thirty years have been built with combinations of three sections: the *verse*, the *chorus*, and the *bridge*. There's so much variety in the way these sections are used that precise, specific definition is nearly impossible.

After examining a number of songs here, however, and later through extended listening on your own, you will develop the ability to intuitively distinguish whether a section of a song is a verse, a chorus, or a bridge. Nevertheless, it's helpful to begin with working definitions so that we can more specifically discuss their many variations.

The Verse

A *verse* in contemporary music can be roughly defined as *the section of a song in which the melody and harmony repeat, but the lyric changes*. It is also generally, but not always, the first part of a song that we hear.

To illustrate the use of the verse, we're going to examine Babyface's song "I'll Make Love to You," which was recorded by Boyz II Men and topped the pop charts for a record-tying fourteen weeks in 1994. The opening section of the song, which begins with the phrase, "Close your eyes, make a wish," is the verse. Illustrated below are the first four bars.

The first verse is immediately followed by a second that begins with the words, "Pour the wine, light the fire." The third and fourth verses, which appear later in the song, begin with the lyrics, "Girl relax, let's go slow," and "Throw your clothes on the floor," respectively. If you listen to the song, you'll notice that although the lyric changes in each of these sections, the basic melody and chordal accompaniment are exactly the same. Sometimes songwriters will repeat all or part of an earlier verse lyrically toward the end of a song, but there will generally be at least two new verses with different lyrics set to the same melody and harmony before that occurs.

The Chorus

Now let's look at the section known as the *chorus*. In contemporary music, a chorus can basically be defined as *the section of the song that repeats musically as well as lyrically*. Although from time to time you will come across a song that has lyric variations in the chorus, at least the words of the basic hook (which we'll discuss later in this chapter) will be repeated along with the melody and harmony. In "I'll Make Love to You" the chorus, which occurs three times in the song (after the second verse, the fourth verse, and the bridge) is the section that begins with the title and ends with the phrase, "And I will not let go till you tell me to."

The Bridge

The *bridge* can generally be defined as *a section that appears only once in a song, both musically and lyrically*. Again, there are sometimes exceptions to this, because certain songs will restate the bridge a second time as part of the arrangement. Another name for the bridge is the *release* because this section usually occurs later in a song and provides melodic and harmonic (as well as lyrical) contrast with the sections that precede it.

In "I'll Make Love to You" the section of the song that begins, "Baby, tonight is your night," is the bridge. It begins on an F# minor 7 chord in contrast to the verse and the chorus, which both begin on the tonic D major chord. From the F# minor 7 it moves directly to a B major chord, which is not found in either of the other sections. Melodically, its range is a step above anything we've heard before and its tessitura (see Chapter 13) is also significantly higher. These harmonic and melodic differences both set the bridge apart from the verse and chorus and enhance its impact on the listener.

Song Forms: Putting the Pieces Together

The way in which a songwriter assembles these sections is known as the *song form*. A song can contain any or all of the building blocks listed above—verse, chorus, and bridge—in many configurations. Let's explore the most common ones and how they've been used successfully.

The Verse-Chorus Song Form

The simplest way in which these various sections are combined is the *verse-chorus form*. A song in this form consists of a verse followed by a chorus, a second verse followed by a chorus, perhaps an instrumental interlude, and then one or more choruses at the end. Occasionally one of the verses (usually the first) is repeated after the instrumental solo and before the final chorus, as in the Doors's classic "Light My Fire." Another common variation is to include a third original verse before the final chorus. Don Henley's "Boys of Summer" (co-written with Mike Campbell), which won him the Grammy for Best Rock Vocal Performance in 1985, and Tim McGraw's 1994 hit "Don't Take the Girl" (written by Craig Martin and Larry Johnson) are examples of songs that use this technique.

Sometimes writers will begin a song with two verses before bringing in the chorus. Sheryl Crow's debut single "Leaving Las Vegas," Janet Jackson's "Let's Wait Awhile," and Peter Cetera's "Glory of Love" (co-written with producer David Foster) are among the many hits that have used this format. On rare occasions, when there is an important story to tell, songwriters will go through three verses before arriving at the chorus, as Don Henley and Glenn Frey do in the Eagles' "Lyin' Eyes." On the other hand, many writers consider getting to the chorus so imperative that they begin with it. This technique can be found in songs in a wide variety of musical idioms ranging from Buddy Holly's "That'll Be the Day" (which was a hit for both Holly and Linda Ronstadt), to Babyface's "Breathe Again," which was a Top 10 hit for Toni Braxton in 1994.

The Verse-Chorus-Bridge Song Form

As we discovered when we were analyzing "I'll Make Love to You," many writers insert a fresh, original *bridge* or *release* section into a song to vary the verse-chorus structure. It will generally follow the second chorus and may itself be either preceded or followed by an instrumental solo. Examples of songs with effective bridges include the Otis Redding/Steve Cropper classic, "Sittin' on the Dock of the Bay," which reached no. 1 for Redding in the '60s and was also a Top 20 hit for Michael Bolton in the '80s (the bridge is the part that begins "Looks like nothing's going to change"), and Mariah Carey and Walter Afanasieff's "Hero" (the bridge is the section that begins "Lord knows dreams are hard to follow").

The Verse-Prechorus-Chorus Song Form

An interesting phenomenon that is occurring more and more frequently these days is the incorporation of a section between the verse and chorus known as the *prechorus*. It is used both to vary the pattern of the verse that precedes it and to prepare the listener for the chorus to come. Other names for the prechorus include the *set-up* (because it sets up the chorus), the *build*, the *B section*, and the *climb*. It provides a melodic and harmonic break from the pattern of the verse and generally ends on a dominant chord (see Chapter 7) that resolves into the first measure of the chorus.

Let's look at how the band Bon Jovi used a prechorus in their 1987 rock and roll hit "Livin' on A Prayer," co-written by Jon Bon Jovi, Richie Sambora, and Desmond Child. The sixteen-measure verse section of the song (the part with the lyric "Tommy used to work on the docks") begins with a flowing melodic eighth-note figure and an Em chord that is sustained for four measures.

The eight-measure prechorus that follows begins with the percussive melodic line illustrated below, which contrasts sharply with the phrasing of the verse melody. In addition, the harmonic rhythm (speed at which chords change) is increased, creating an intensity that finally explodes into the chorus.

Among the many songs that make use of a prechorus are Vince Gill's "I Still Believe in You" (co-written with John Jarvis), Billy Ocean's "Caribbean Queen" (co-written with Kieth Diamond), and Brian Adams' "Please Forgive Me" (co-written with Mutt Lange). Often songs that have a prechorus such as "Livin' on A Prayer" and "I Still Believe in You" do not have a bridge, since the prechorus creates sufficient variety from the verse-chorus format. However, some songs such as "Please Forgive Me" have a bridge after the second chorus as well as a prechorus preceding each chorus.

Again, there are no hard-and-fast rules about how these different sections are used in writing. At this stage it is only important for you to be able to recognize them, so that as we refer to them throughout the rest of the book, you have a clear understanding of how the melodic, harmonic, and rhythmic techniques we'll be studying fit into the basic structure of a song.

The Verse-Verse-Bridge-Verse (Or A-A-B-A) Song Form

While the vast majority of songs that have topped the charts in the last twenty years have used one of the variations of the verse-chorus form discussed above, this has not always been the case. In the '30s, '40s, and well into the '50s, most contemporary popular songs were in a form known as the *A-A-B-A*, or *verse-verse-bridge-verse*. Instead of a chorus, this form contains a verse, a second verse, a bridge or release, and a concluding verse. The bridge or release is generally longer than the bridge in the verse-chorus form and provides the only contrast with the repeated verses.

A well-known example of this form in today's music is Billy Joel's "Shameless," which was a hit both for him and for Garth Brooks. The verses, which are the sections beginning with the title, are written in the key of G and use primarily chords that are drawn from the G scale (or diatonic [see Chapter 7] to the key of G). The bridge, however, uses $B\flat$, $A\flat$, and $E\flat$ chords within the first four measures as well as melodic phrases that are substantially longer than those in the verse.

Although songs such as "Shameless," Whitney Houston's "Saving All My Love for You" (co-written by Michael Masser and Gerry Goffin), and Richard Marx's 1993 hit "Now and Forever" are quite modern in their sound, with some changes in arrangement and orchestration they could very easily be played alongside standards such as "God Bless the Child," "Misty," or "Georgia on My Mind," all of which use the same A-A-B-A structure.

This form, however, is not necessarily limited to traditional-sounding ballads. Successful rock tunes—such as the Beatles' "Hey Jude" and Bruce Springsteen's 1994 Oscar-winning hit "Streets of Philadelphia"—are also chorusless A-A-B-A songs. In addition, two of our most prolific and successful pop writers, Billy Joel and Stevie Wonder, are extremely fond of this form and have used it extensively. Stevie's "You Are the Sunshine of My Life," "Another Star," and

"Part-Time Lover" and Billy Joel's "Just the Way You Are," "An Innocent Man," and "Still Rock 'n' Roll to Me" (in addition to "Shameless") are but a few examples of the ways in which these composers have added to the rich legacy of A-A-B-A songs in the history of contemporary popular music.

Variations on the A-A-B-A Song Form

Back in the '40s and '50s, two-and-a-half to three minutes was the standard time for a single recording, but more recently we have come to expect three-, four-, and even five-minute songs on the charts. Because of the brevity of the A-A-B-A form and the lack of a repeated chorus that can be used as part of a "fade" ending (see Chapter 20), writers have often chosen to expand this form in various ways. These include instrumental solos on the verse section ("Shameless") or bridge section ("Still Rock 'n' Roll to Me"), repeating one or more sections ("Another Star"), or repeating the bridge section with different lyrics ("Hey Jude").

This last technique may seem a bit confusing for those of you who are taking your first look at analyzing contemporary song forms through the examples in this chapter, because my original definition of "bridge" was a section that never repeats. However, once you get the feeling of what a verse, chorus, and bridge are, you will be able to clearly differentiate between a bridge with new lyrics and a verse.

Less Common Song Forms

Before we complete our study of song forms, we should look at some others that, while used only rarely, still have been responsible for several hits on the charts. The most common of these is the A-A-A, which simply consists of several (usually three) repeated verses. Two successful examples of songs in this form are Amanda McBroom's Oscar-nominated "The Rose," recorded by Bette Midler, and Toni Wine and Carole Bayer Sager's "A Groovy Kind of Love," which was a hit both for Wayne Fontana and the Mindbenders in 1966 and Phil Collins in 1988.

In 1984, Sting (Gordon Sumner) of The Police took home a Grammy for Song of the Year with his hypnotic "Every Breath You Take." This song altered the standard A-A-B-A form by adding a new

"C" section after the third verse (with the lyric "Since you've gone I've been lost without a trace"), making the form A-A-B-A-C-B-A. In 1993, Janet Jackson and co-writers Jimmy Jam and Terry Lewis garnered an Oscar nomination and a number 1 hit for their song "Again" from the motion picture *Poetic Justice*. This song features three distinct sections that repeat in order (verse-chorus-bridge, verse-chorus-bridge) with the verse only half as long the second time, followed by another half verse, a chorus with altered lyrics, and a concluding section (that begins, "Hold me, hold me") which is based harmonically on the verse but has a completely different melody. Experienced writers like these often take such liberties with traditional forms, but it would be a good idea for you to first become familiar with the conventional usages before trying such adventurous variations.

> Before going on to the rest of the chapter, listen to five of your all-time favorite songs and five songs you like that are currently being played on the radio. Write out the lyrics (and music, if you're able to) and then analyze the structure in terms of verses, choruses, bridges, and prechoruses, if any.

The Hook

Perhaps the most important word in the songwriter's vocabulary, at least in the realm of song structure, is the term "hook." The *hook*, which generally contains the song's title, is *the part of the song that is repeated frequently and therefore tends to remain in the mind of the listener.* Or, you might say, it is the part that you're left "hooked" on or left singing after the song is complete.

In most songs, particularly those with a verse-chorus form, the melodic, harmonic, and rhythmic components of the hook are crucial. A hook should have a melody that is original and memorable, and yet at the same time is easily singable. That melody should be accompanied by a fresh and interesting harmony and an instrumental arrangement that is compatible yet distinctive in its own right. A good example is the hook of Bon Jovi's "Livin' on A Prayer," whose prechorus we examined earlier in this chapter.

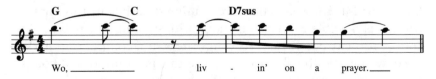

Notice that the melody reaches high C, which is a full fourth higher than the melody of either the verse or the prechorus, both of which peak at G. In addition, both the G chord and the D7sus4 chord are heard here for the first time. Yet, although the melody and harmony break new ground, they have that familiar, singable quality the first time you hear them that makes for a successful hook.

Placement of the Hook

As we have seen, Bon Jovi set up the hook of "Livin' on A Prayer" to be quite memorable, yet one thing about it is slightly unusual. It first occurs at the end of the second line of the chorus. While this hook placement does not interfere with our remembering it or being able to sing it in our minds long after the song is completed, it is not the most common placement. The hook in a verse-chorus form is usually found either at the beginning of the chorus (as in "Caribbean Queen"), the end of the chorus (as in "Breathe Again"), or both (as in "I Still Believe in You"). Very often, the hook will be repeated more than once. "Livin' on A Prayer" uses it at the end of both the second and fourth lines, while "I'll Make Love to You" uses it at the beginning of the first and the third lines.

While the hook is generally less important in an A-A-B-A song than in one with a verse-chorus structure, it is still the part of the song that sticks in our minds and usually contains the title. In this form, the hook is typically placed at the beginning of the verse, as in "Shameless," or at the end, as in "Just the Way You Are." Occasionally you will find the title of an A-A-B-A song in a different place, as in another Vince Gill hit, "Look at Us" (co-written with Max Barnes), where it occurs at *both* the beginning and end of the verse, or in Billy Vera's "At This Moment," where it occurs at the *end* of the first line of every verse.

In Chapters 13–15, we'll be delving much more deeply into the melodic considerations that make a hook memorable and singable, as well as how the hook relates to the rest of the section in which it is found. For now it is important only that you can identify it and place it within the song structures outlined earlier in this chapter. While it is possible to write a hit song without a hook (such as "The Rose"), it is extremely rare. As songwriters in a competitive marketplace, we need to be able to recognize this most important component of today's music and use it effectively in our own writing.

Go through the songs you selected previously and identify the hook in each one. Notice where it occurs and, if it is a verse-chorus song, how many times it occurs within the chorus. Put copies of these songs aside so that as you continue through this book you can analyze their harmonies, melodies, and rhythms in the context of the information presented in subsequent chapters.

Wrap-Up

In this chapter we have examined the song forms contemporary writers from Buddy Holly and Billy Joel to Janet Jackson and Vince Gill have used as the structures for their hits. We have looked at the many variations of the verse-chorus form (including those that contain bridges and prechoruses) as well as the A-A-B-A form. We have also discussed the importance of hooks as well as the possibilities for their placement within the song structure. Be certain that you have a thorough understanding of these terms before going on, as we'll be referring to them frequently throughout the rest of the book.

Prosody and Contrast
Secrets of Songwriting Success

How many times have you listened to a song and said to yourself, "This tune is great; it really moves me"? On the other hand, how many times have you listened to a song, perhaps on a similar theme or in a similar style, and said, "This is good, but it doesn't really knock me out"? What makes the difference? Of course, if it could be reduced to a simple formula, all of us would be writing award-winning songs year after year, and not just the Elton Johns, Babyfaces, and Diane Warrens.

Yet in the hundreds and hundreds of "great" songs I've analyzed with my students through the years, two elements have consistently been present. In the workshops I teach around the country, I refer to these concepts, known as *prosody* and *contrast*, as the "secrets of songwriting success." I am introducing them at this point so they will be part of our vocabulary as we delve into the various aspects of pop musical composition in subsequent chapters.

Prosody

Have you ever been at the movies and, as the hero or heroine was walking down the street, suddenly gotten a feeling that something terrible was going to spring from behind that corner he or she was approaching? Most likely it was the score, or musical accompaniment of the movie, that evoked this feeling. The music suddenly shifted from simple and nondescript (or perhaps no music at all) to an ominous melody or series of chords. In this way, the musical accompaniment underscored the action taking place on the screen.

As pop composers, whether we write our own lyrics or collaborate with others, we are basically film scorers—and the film we are scoring is the lyric message of the song. If the lyric expresses how happy the singer and her lover are in their relationship, the use of slow, mournful music would be terribly inappropriate. Similarly, if the singer were singing about how angry she was at someone who had not treated her fairly, a lilting melody and serene harmony would be equally inappropriate. This marriage of music and lyric in emotional tone is what I refer to as *prosody*.

Randy Sharp, who has written hits for Alabama, Patty Loveless, Restless Heart, and many others, described prosody in this way: "If the intent of a lyric and the whole presentation is a specific emotional response from the listener, then the music takes a big part of that burden. You can write the most emotionally drenching lyric in the world, but if the music isn't appropriate, it's not going to work. People listen to Tchaikovsky and other classical masters and can see the scene and the story without any words. A good song should pass this test as well. You may not know the specifics, but you should know emotionally what is going on because the music carries that information on its own."

When discussing prosody, please bear in mind that in classical theory it is more narrowly defined as singing the words in the way that they are spoken. For example, if you were writing music to a lyric that included the word "sympathy," you would see to it that the melodic accent was on the first syllable so the word was pronounced "SYM-pa-thy" rather than "sym-PA-thy." While this more narrow meaning of prosody is extremely important in songwriting as well, I have chosen to use the word in a much larger context. One could perhaps call what I am referring to as "emotional prosody," which would incorporate the way that the harmony and underlying groove of the song as well as the melody underscore the meaning of the lyric. Remember that when I use the word "prosody" throughout this chapter and the rest of the book, I am using it in this broader meaning.

Melodic Prosody

A well-known German film composer and music educator used to always tell his students, "Remember—up is happy, down is sad." While there are occasional exceptions to this rule, it also tends to hold true in most successful pop songs. The opening ascending melody of Jimmy Webb's classic "Up, Up and Away," recorded by the Fifth Dimension, and the first measures of the chorus of "Up Where We Belong" from the film *An Officer and a Gentleman* (music by Jack Nitsche and Buffy Sainte-Marie with lyrics by Will Jennings) are classic cases in point. Similarly, the descending melody (illustrated below) in the opening line of the chorus of Alan Rich and Jud Friedman's "I Don't Have the Heart," which was a number 1 hit for James Ingram in 1990, emotionally reinforces the singer's sadness at not being able to give the woman to whom he is singing the kind of love she wants.

Prosody in Harmony and Rhythm

It is not only the melody that creates prosody in a song, however. In the case of "Up Where We Belong," when the melody rises, the bass line moves upward from D to F♯ to G as well. In addition, certain chords tend to communicate more bright and happy emotions, while others tend to have a more melancholy or poignant effect. Perhaps the classic example of this is found in Carole King's "You've Got a Friend." In the verse where she sings, "When you're down and troubled . . . and nothing, nothing is going right," the harmonic accompaniment is in a minor key. As the tone of the song shifts in the chorus with the lyrics, "You just call out my name and you know wherever I am I'll come running," the harmony shifts to a brighter, more positive major key.

Rhythm can also be used to create prosody. When was the last time you heard a song with a lyric about being out on the dance floor played in a relaxed, romantic tempo? How inappropriate would it be to set a song such as Wynonna's "My Strongest Weakness" to a bright, bouncy rhythm track or to hear the Pointer Sisters' "I'm So Excited" set to a slow ballad tempo? We will be discussing specifically how melody, harmony, and rhythm can affect the prosody of the song in greater detail in subsequent chapters. At this point it is only important that you be aware of what emotional prosody is and the impact it can have.

Contrast

Listen! This is important! It affects your songwriting! One of the most effective ways to maintain a listener's attention throughout a song (without which the song can never become a hit) is by using a device known as *contrast*. A perfect case in point is how much attention you paid to the previous sentence. If that sentence had been buried somewhere in the middle of this paragraph amid sentences of its own length and similar structure, there's a good chance you would have glossed over it and missed its importance. After reading the prior three short exclamatory sentences, however, you were much more receptive to reading one of long duration because it *contrasted* with what had gone before.

The importance of contrast in today's music was perhaps most dramatically expressed by those celebrated teenage music critics of the '90s: Beavis and Butthead. Upon listening to the chorus of a full-on headbanging heavy metal tune on their MTV show one night, Beavis tells his partner, "Wow, this is cool." When the song shifts to a more melodic verse, however, he says to Butthead, "Ugh, this part sucks." Butthead, in his infinite wisdom, then turns to Beavis and replies, "Yeah, but if they didn't have a part that sucked, the part that's cool wouldn't sound as cool."

While we may not elicit such explicit reactions as this from our listeners, it's basically true that people tend to lose interest when the same thing is repeated over and over again. As songwriters, what we hate to hear most when we're submitting material for a project are comments like "This sounds good, but it really doesn't stand out" or "This is well written, but it just doesn't have that special something." The effective use of contrast can make a big difference by enabling us to keep our songs fresh and original, while still sounding familiar enough to sing along with on first listening.

Melodic Contrast

Just as melody, harmony, and rhythm—the three basic musical components of pop songwriting—are the areas in which we can create prosody, they're also the areas in which we can create contrast. We discussed an excellent example of melodic contrast in Chapter 2 when we analyzed Bon Jovi's "Livin' on a Prayer." Notice how the staccato accentuated rhythm of the prechorus section ("We've gotta hold on to what we've got") contrasts with the flowing eighth-note melodies of the verse. Although the melodic rhythm remains similar in the chorus, there is a contrast in *melodic range*, because the melody (as we mentioned) rises a full fourth higher than it does in either of the two preceding sections. This holds the listener's attention so that as the song proceeds through its verse to prechorus to chorus development, we are constantly hearing fresh melodic ideas.

Harmonic Contrast

A song that strongly illustrates the use of harmonic contrast is Don Henley's 1989 hit "The End of the Innocence" (co-written with Bruce Hornsby), which earned him a Grammy for Best Rock Vocal Performance. The entire verse consists, with one exception, of A♭, D♭, and E♭ major chords that last for one or two measures each. Now look at the first four measures of the prechorus.

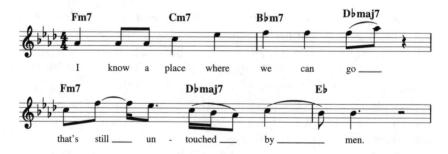

Henley and Hornsby create three distinct types of harmonic contrast in this section. First, they make frequent use of minor chords (four in three measures) as opposed to the major chords that predominate in the verse. They also employ four-part minor and major *seventh* chords (see Chapter 6) compared to the triads used exclusively in the previous section. The final example of contrast is a change in the *harmonic rhythm*, or number of chords per measure.

Notice that the first three bars of the prechorus contain two chords each, while in the beginning of the verse each chord lasts for two full measures. These harmonic variations make the prechorus sound more fresh and interesting, and contribute significantly to making it a classic song.

Rhythmic Contrast

The rhythm, or groove of a song, is the third area in which we can create effective contrast. Sometimes this may be very obvious, as in the case of Meat Loaf's "I'd Do Anything for Love" (by Jim Steinman), in which the verse section ("Some days it don't come easy") is more than fifty beats per minute faster than the chorus. Or it can be as subtle as the difference between the first verse of Counting Crows' debut single "'Round Here," where Adam Duritz's vocal is supported only by the sparsely arpegiatted guitar of his co-writer David Bryson, and the second verse, where the bass and drums are laying down a solid groove under the guitar and keyboards. (Grooves and instrumentation will be discussed in detail in Chapters 19 and 20.)

> Choose two or three of the songs you selected for the exercise in Chapter 2. See if you can find at least one clear, specific example of either prosody or contrast in each of them.

Wrap-Up

As we have seen, prosody and contrast are key elements in the craft of successful songwriting. They often make the difference between a tune that is "just okay" and one that may become a hit or even a standard. As we continue to examine segments from various songs throughout the rest of the book, be aware of these two important elements and the impact that they have on the listener.

Part Two

Theory: The Fundamentals

4

Reading Music
Pitches and Note Values

Before embarking on our journey into the world of harmony, melody, and rhythm in contemporary music, we need to spend some time learning the language we'll be using to discuss them. While it is not absolutely necessary to be able to read and write music to create a song, the majority of today's most successful songwriters are well versed in these skills. Tom Snow, several of whose hits we're going to be looking at in subsequent chapters (including "Let's Hear It for the Boy," "He's So Shy," Bonnie Raitt's "Love Sneakin' Up On You," and Selena's "Dreaming of You"), put it best when he said, "I find that my formal music education is enormously important, because the theoretical understanding it gave me enables me to expand in different directions as my career progresses. I feel like I've got real longevity because of it. I'm not limited to one style of writing."

It is also essential for us to have this common language of written music to proceed with the work in this book. Just as you would need to read French in order to study French literature, if you want to *study* music, you need to speak the *language* of music.

Those of you who are already familiar with the fundamentals of theory will want to skim over the next three chapters as a review. If you have a limited theory background, these chapters will help clarify the specific areas that apply to songwriting. For those with no experience whatsoever, these chapters will serve as a valid introduction, but it's highly recommended that you take a basic music course as well. Music is not like history or mathematics where the actual printed words or symbols are the full content of what you're studying. Notes in music are only *visual representations of sound,* and unless you can accurately make the connection between the visual symbols and the sounds they represent, you won't be able to successfully apply what you learn to your songwriting. Having spent many years as a professional musician, I can personally attest to this. Like Tom Snow, I received a wonderful education in music school, but much of the learning I did "on the job," where a direct and immediate aural connection to the written music was always present, has been even more valuable.

Placing Notes on the Staff

The notes that create music occur, like everything else, in both time and space. The location of a note in space is musically referred to as its *pitch.* Its location in time is called its *duration* or *value.*

Pitches are notated musically on a *staff,* a ladderlike device that indicates their relative highness or lowness. As notes get higher on the staff, their pitches go up; as they get lower, their pitches descend. A symbol called a *clef* is inserted at the beginning of the staff to specifically identify the pitches. Although many clefs are used in musical notation, the two most common are the *treble* or *G clef* and the *bass* or *F clef.*

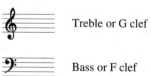

Treble or G clef

Bass or F clef

The musical alphabet uses the first seven letters of the English alphabet, A through G, after which these seven letters repeat. The G is located on the second line from the bottom of the treble staff (where the clef sign curls over). This is one reason why it is called the G clef. Each line or space is assigned the next letter name above or below G. Therefore, the notes on the treble staff look like this.

Notice that the notes on the lines spell out E–G–B–D–F, which can stand for Every Good Boy Does Fine. (The British version of this, Every Good Boy Deserves Favour, was once used as an album title by the Moody Blues.) The spaces, F–A–C–E, spell out the word "face." While these devices can be helpful in the beginning of your study, it is best to memorize the location of each individual note as soon as possible so that, for example, the symbol illustrated below becomes as readily recognizable to you as does the letter "G."

In the bass clef, notes are placed on the lines and spaces as follows.

While it is important to be familiar with at least these two clefs to read and write music, we will primarily be illustrating our work on the treble clef, except for the references to bass lines in Chapter 20. Those of you who are more experienced in reading bass clef—such as bass, cello, or trombone players—may wish to make the appropriate transpositions as we proceed.

To write a particular melody or spell a particular chord, it often is necessary to use notes above or below the staff. In this case, we use what are known as *ledger lines*. Each ledger line and space it creates represents another letter name up or down the staff. In the treble clef, the additional notes look like this.

If we want to raise or lower pitches a half-step, we add a sharp (♯) or flat (♭). A third symbol, called a natural (♮) is used to cancel out a sharp or a flat. I will make the exact meaning of raising or lowering a half-step clear later in this chapter, but for now you need only learn to recognize these symbols. On the staff they look like this.

| G | G sharp | G flat | G natural |

Notice that the symbols for sharp, flat, and natural are placed on the staff *before* the note. This is done so that musicians reading the music will know whether the note is sharp or flat before they play it.

I strongly recommend that you take the time now to become so familiar with the location of these notes on the treble staff that you can recognize them as easily as the actual letters by which they are named. There are, as a former music teacher of mine once suggested, two excellent ways to do this: practice and more practice. I suggest you buy a book of sheet music and literally "read" it through from cover to cover, naming all the notes as they appear on the treble staff. You might also wish to make up a series of flash cards of these notes and carry them around with you. It's a great way to pass the time waiting at the doctor's office or in line at the bank, and in a matter of a week or two you'll be very "sharp" at recognizing these notes, and they'll become quite "natural" to you.

The Twelve Notes

The distance between a note and its next highest repetition (for example, between an A and the next highest A) is called an *octave,* because "oct" is the Latin prefix for eight (as in *oct*agon), and there are eight letter names between a note and its octave.

| A | B | C | D | E | F | G | A |

There are, however, twelve distinct notes or pitches between A and A. They are A, A♯ or B♭, B, C, C♯ or D♭, D, D♯ or E♭, E, F, F♯ or G♭, G, and G♯ or A♭. The distance between each of these notes and the next is called a *half-step*. Thus, there are twelve half-steps in an octave. Notice that the distance between each of the natural notes is a whole step, with the exception of B and C and E and F, each of which are a half-step apart. Thus, an A♯ would be a note one half-step above A, but a B♯ would be the same as the note C. Similarly, an E♭ is one half-step below E, but an F♭ is the same as an E natural. While this may seem a bit confusing at first to those of you who are beginners, it becomes very simple when looking at the keyboard.

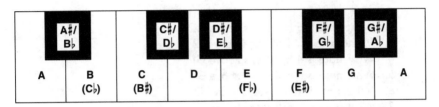

Guitarists may find this a bit more difficult to grasp, because the guitar fingerboard is not as easy to visually comprehend as the piano keyboard. On the guitar, each fret above the open string represents a half-step, or one pitch. Thus, the open A or fifth string is the note A. Fingered on the first fret, it becomes A♯ or B♭. Fingered on the second fret, it becomes B; on the third fret, C; and so on, as illustrated below.

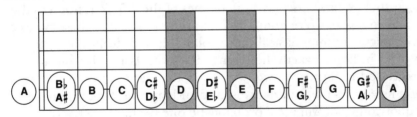

An excellent aid to perceiving these relationships on the guitar is Andrew Caponigro's *The Fingerboard Workbook*, published by G. Schirmer, which I highly recommend to all guitarist/songwriters. But whether you write primarily on keyboard or guitar, you'll need to be familiar with the location of notes on the staff, understand their half-step relationships, and have the ability to play them on your instrument in order to incorporate the rest of the work we'll be doing in this book into your songwriting.

On a piece of staff paper (paper with preprinted music staves, available at most music stores), write the answers to the following questions. Write all the possible variations of each letter name answer that fall between F below the treble staff and E above. The first one has been completed for you as an example. When you have finished, compare your answers with those in the appendix and play each note on your instrument.

I. What note is 4 half-steps above E?

G#/Ab

2. What note is 5 half-steps below B?
3. What note is 2 half-steps above F?
4. What note is 4 half-steps above G?
5. What note is 3 half-steps above Bb?
6. What note is 6 half-steps above D?
7. What note is 2 half-steps below C#?
8. What note is 3 half-steps below C?
9. What note is I half-step above E?
10. What note is 7 half-steps below F#?
11. What note is 5 half-steps above Db?
12. What note is 4 half-steps above A?

Rhythmic Values

Now that we have discussed the pitches of the different notes as they occur in space, we're going to look at the *duration* of these notes as they occur in time. Basically, the color (black or white) and stem of a note indicate exactly how long that note lasts. This duration is expressed in terms of *beats*, which are the basic pulses of a song. If you listen to a piece of dance music and tap your foot in time, each tap of your foot will most probably be one beat.

Five types of notes are commonly used in contemporary music. The first of these is the whole note, which lasts 4 beats in 4/4 time. (We'll be explaining exactly what 4/4 time means later in this chapter.) The next is the half note, which lasts 2 beats. The other common notes are the quarter note, which lasts 1 beat, the eighth note, which lasts a half beat, and the sixteenth note, which lasts a quarter of a beat. These notes are illustrated below on the pitch of G. Notice that when there is more than one eighth or sixteenth note they are joined by a beam and look different from a single note.

Whole   Half   Quarter Eighth   Sixteenth

It is difficult to get a true sense of what these note values sound like from the printed page of a book alone. If you have not had any previous experience with written music, I wholeheartedly recommend either having a friend play them for you or taking an applied theory or ear-training course to get a better sense of their actual *sound*.

Whole and half notes are of longer duration and are generally referred to as *sustained* notes. Whole notes frequently occur at the end of ballads such as Alex Worth and Hy Zaret's "Unchained Melody," recorded by both Willie Nelson and the Righteous Brothers (whose version was featured as the love theme in the hit movie *Ghost*). To get an idea of the sound of half notes, think of the notes accompanying the words "see" and "you" in the hook of Diane Warren's "When I See You Smile," which was a number 1 hit for the band Bad English in 1989.

Because quarter notes last exactly one beat and the beat represents the basic pulse of the song, quarter notes fall exactly on each pulse. An example of this is the opening measure of John Williams' "Can You Read My Mind?" (love theme from *Superman*) illustrated below, with lyrics by Leslie Bricusse.

Eighth notes, like quarter notes, fall regularly within the rhythmic pattern of a song, except that there are two eighth notes for every beat. Remember the opening notes of Pam Tillis, Bob DiPiero, and Jan Buckingham's "Cleopatra, Queen of Denial" ("I said he had a lot of . . .") or the hook of Toni Tenille's "Do That to Me One More Time," and the sound of eighth notes will come readily to mind.

Sixteenth notes last half as long as eighth notes, because there are four of them to each beat. Some examples are the first three notes of the hook of Rod Temperton's "Give Me the Night" (as recorded by George Benson) and the opening eight notes of Chris DeBurgh's 1987 top ten hit, "The Lady in Red" ("I've never seen you looking so . . .").

Extending Note Values

All of the basic note values, from whole notes to sixteenth notes, may be augmented by half their value through the addition of a dot.

Thus, a dotted half note would receive three beats, a dotted quarter note one and a half beats, a dotted eighth note three-quarters of a beat (half a beat plus half again of that), etc. If the songwriter wants *no* note to sound for a period of time, a device known as a *rest* is used. Rests come in the same set of values as notes: whole, half, quarter, eighth, and sixteenth.

Whole Rest · Half Rest · Quarter Rest · Eighth Rest · Sixteenth Rest

You will notice that, because these rests represent the absence of any musical pitch, they are not written on a particular line or space of the staff. An exception to this are whole and half rests, which are traditionally written within the third space, though they have nothing to do with the note "C." Look back at "Can You Read My Mind?" on page 33; you'll notice an example of both a dotted note (the dotted half on F at the beginning of the second measure) and a rest (the quarter rest at the end of the measure). Of course, most contemporary songs do not use these notes in isolated configurations like the ones I have referred to. Melodies are usually a combination of whole, half, quarter, eighth, and sixteenth notes and rests in various rhythmic combinations. Indeed, it is these very combinations that often give melodic hooks their distinctive characteristics. (See Chapter 14 for a more extensive discussion of this principle.)

Another device used by music writers is placing three notes within the normal duration of two. Such notes are called *triplets* and are indicated by placing a bracket and the numeral "3" over the notes involved, as in the third measure of the Lennon/McCartney classic "Strawberry Fields Forever," illustrated below:

Let me take you down — cause I'm go-in' to ___ Straw-ber-ry Fields

Notice that in this case the triplet sign is over three quarter notes (accompanying the lyric "Strawberry"). These quarter notes are played in a "3 against 2" pattern and take up the same space as two quarter notes normally would. Triplets can also freely be used with eighth notes (three eighth note triplets to a beat), sixteenth notes (six sixteenth note triplets to a beat), or even half notes.

Measures and Time Signatures

As you'll notice in all the musical examples we have looked at so far, groups of notes are separated by vertical lines, which we call *bar lines.* These bar lines divide music into units of time of equal duration known as *bars* or *measures.*

At the beginning of each piece of music is a set of two numbers written with one number directly above the other, called the *time signature.* The top number indicates the number of beats per measure, and the lower number indicates what type of note (usually quarter, eighth, or half) is given one beat. Thus, in $4/4$ time (the time signature of more than 90 percent of contemporary songs), there are four beats in every measure and a quarter note is given one beat.

Another frequently used time signature is $3/4$ time, sometimes called waltz time, where there are three beats per measure. Examples of well-known songs in $3/4$ time include Angela Kaset's "Something in Red" (a 1992 hit for Lorrie Morgan), the verse of the Beatles's classic "Lucy in the Sky with Diamonds" (the chorus is in $4/4$ time), and Paul Gordon and Jay Gruska's "Friends and Lovers," which was recorded both as a pop duet by Gloria Loring and Carl Anderson and as a country duet by Eddie Rabbitt and Juice Newton.

In songs written in $4/4$ or $3/4$ time (and the rare song in $7/4$ time such as Pink Floyd's "Money" or $5/4$ time like Dave Brubeck's "Take Five"), each quarter note is subdivided into *two* eighth notes. There is another type of meter in which each quarter note is subdivided into *three* eighth notes. Because it is awkward and cumbersome to write an extensive series of triplets, the time signature is usually expressed in terms of eighth notes, either $12/8$ (twelve eighth notes per measure), $9/8$ (nine eighth notes per measure), or $6/8$ (six eighth notes per measure). Songs with this meter are found in a wide variety of styles, ranging from Seal's 1996 Grammy winner for both Song and Record of the Year "Kiss From a Rose" and Stephen Sondheim's "Send in the Clowns" (both of which alternate between $12/8$ and $9/8$ time) to rock hits like Aerosmith's "Crazy" and R.E.M.'s "Everybody Hurts." In Chapter 19 there will be a more extensive discussion of the different rhythmic grooves associated with this type of subdivision.

Often in the process of writing melodies, you will want to use a melody note that begins in one measure and ends in the next. To do this, you need to use a device called a *tie*, which joins the heads of the respective notes. One important use of this device is to indicate what we call a rhythmic anticipation or *push* where a note is brought in a half-beat early to "push" the melody forward. We can find two examples of this in "Strawberry Fields Forever" (illustrated on page 34) on the words "down" and "to." Try playing the melody without these anticipations (make the "C" accompanying the lyric "you" and the "A" accompanying the syllable "-in" dotted quarter notes and place the words "down" and "to" directly on the first beats of the following measures) and listen to the difference between the anticipated and nonanticipated versions.

> Choose two or three of the songs that you previously selected that have relatively simple melodies and for which you have records or tapes. Play them through and first count the number of measures, then see if you can write out the melodic rhythm (note values only, not pitches) of the first 8 bars of each melody. If you can get sheet music for these songs, compare what you have written with the actual note values, and see if you understand any discrepancies.

Wrap-Up

In this chapter we have covered some of the basics of note location (pitch) and note duration (value). While this outline is not a substitute for the many years that most accomplished musicians have spent integrating this knowledge, it should at least give those of you with no formal musical education enough of a background to absorb and understand the information presented in subsequent chapters. As I mentioned earlier, it is extremely difficult to convey the essence of this material from the printed page alone, and I heartily recommend that those of you who are musical beginners take a class with a competent teacher to augment your familiarity with the *sound* that musical symbols represent. Remember, theoretical understanding alone will do you absolutely no good when you're staring at that blank sheet of paper with the intention of writing a song. It is only as these melodic and rhythmic (and in later chapters, harmonic) concepts are incorporated into what you *hear* that you will get maximum value from this study.

5

Major Scales and Intervals

In Chapter 4, we examined how notes are located in space (pitch) and time (duration). In this chapter we're going to focus on particular groupings of pitches known as major scales. These scales are important not only because the melodies of most of the songs we hear on the radio are built on them, but also because the chords used to harmonize those melodies are derived from them as well. We'll learn both the traditional method of constructing major scales and a unique shortcut that will enable you to memorize them in a matter of days. We're also going to look at two other important aspects of music theory, known as *key signatures* and *intervals*.

Major Scales

A *major scale* can be defined as *a series of pitches that are separated by half-steps in a pattern of 2–2–1–2–2–2–1*, or whole step (two half-steps), whole step, half-step, whole step, whole step, whole step, half-step. Thus, if the root (note upon which the scale is built) of a major scale is C, the next note in the scale will be D, because D is two half-steps (one whole step) above C. The next note will be E, because E is two half-steps up from D. The fourth note in the scale will be F, because F is one half-step above E (remember that all of the natural notes are separated by two half-steps *except* for E and F and B and C; see the piano keyboard illustration on page 31 or the guitar fingerboard illustration on page 31). The rest of the notes in the scale will be G (two half-steps above F), A (two half-steps above G), B (two half-steps above A), and finally a return to C (the root) one half-step above B. These notes form what we call the C-major scale, illustrated below. Sing this scale or play it on your instrument to get an idea of its sound before you continue.

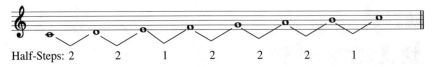

Half-Steps: 2   2   1   2   2   2   1

Although all major scales have the same relative sound, the C-major scale is unique in that it is the only one that contains all natural notes (no sharps or flats). The others each have one or more *accidentals,* a term that includes both sharps and flats (much as the term "siblings" refers to both brothers and sisters). When writing out the other major scales, it is important to know which accidental (the sharp or the flat) to use for notes that are not natural. To determine this, we follow a very important rule: *Every major scale has one and only one of every letter name.* This means that every scale will have some sort of D, whether it is D, D♯, or D♭. It will never have two of these, nor will it ever have none. Similarly, every major scale will have at least one E, F, G, A, etc., whether the note is sharp, flat, or natural.

Let's see how this applies, for example, to a B♭-major scale. The first note in this scale is, of course, the root B♭. The next notes are C (two half-steps above B♭), and D, which is two half-steps up from C. The fourth note will require an accidental, because the pitch one half-step above D is D♯ or E♭. In this particular situation, we will name it E♭, because we already have a D natural in the scale (the third note). Notice also that the next pitch above E♭ is the note two half-steps higher, or F. If we used a D♯ to represent the fourth degree of the scale, we would have two Ds and no Es. Therefore, we call the note E♭.

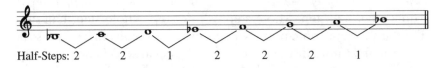

Half-Steps: 2   2   1   2   2   2   1

Before going on to the rest of this chapter, write out the D, F, A♭, and B-major scales on staff paper and play or sing them. Remember to use accidentals so that each scale comes out having one and *only* one of every letter name. Compare your results with those in the appendix.

Identifying Major Scales: A Shortcut

The way I have just explained major scales is the way they are generally taught in most music schools. Rapid recall of these scales is important, because all the rest of the topics we will discuss in this book—from chords to melodies, even to minor scales—are derived from them. However, I have found memorization using this method to be a difficult and tedious process. I'm now going to give you a much more efficient system for memorizing these scales, which has enabled virtually every student who has worked with me over the years to be fluent with them in a matter of a week or two. It is based on asking yourself three simple questions and knowing the answer to each question.

The first question you need to ask yourself is, *"Is the scale I'm dealing with sharp or flat?"* You'll notice from the examples you worked out above that all major scales have either sharps or flats, never both (with the exception of the C-major scale, which has neither sharps nor flats). Scales that have sharps are referred to as sharp scales, while scales that have flats are referred to as flat scales. Any scale with a sharp in its name, such as F♯ or C♯, is going to be a sharp scale. Similarly, any scale with a flat in its name, such as B♭ or E♭, will obviously be a flat scale. The only ones in question are those that have as their root a natural note such as A or B. In those cases the rule is: F is Flat, the rest are sharp. So, for example, A, D, G, and B are sharp scales because F is the only scale with a natural note as its root that is flat.

The second question you need to ask yourself is, *"How many sharps or flats are in this scale?"* You can answer that question by memorizing a simple series of letters that form the acronym GDAEBF. The way this acronym works is that the number of sharps in sharp scales proceeds from left to right, while the number of flats in flat scales proceeds from right to left. Therefore G, a sharp scale, has one sharp because G is the first letter in the acronym. Similarly, D has two sharps, A three sharps, etc. F, the first flat scale, has one flat; B♭, because it is the second scale reading from right to left, has two flats, and so on.

The best way to memorize this particular acronym is to create a series of words of which G-D-A-E-B-F are the first letters. The one my students generally use is "Good Dogs Are Everyone's Best Friends." However, feel free to be creative and make up your own.

The third and final question we need to ask ourselves is, *"Which sharps or flats are in this scale?"* The answer to this question is in the form of another acronym, FCGDAEB, with sharps again reading from left to right and flats from right to left. Thus, if a scale has one sharp, it will be F♯. If a scale contains two sharps, they will be F♯ and C♯, and so on up to six sharps. Reading the diagram from right to left, if a scale has one flat, it will be B♭. If a scale contains two flats, they will be B♭ and E♭, and so on up to six flats.

I recommend you also memorize this acronym by associating it with a series of words that have its letters as their initials. The basic one I use with my students is "Fat Cats Go Down Alleys Eating Birds." As before, though, I invite you to be creative and come up with something that will help *you* remember it more easily. To summarize, then, the system I have presented looks as follows:

1. *Does the scale have sharps or flats?* **F** has **F**lats (other scales with natural note roots have sharps).
2. *How many sharps or flats are in the scale?*

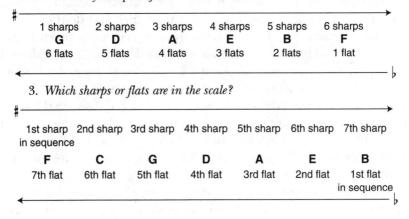

3. *Which sharps or flats are in the scale?*

Applying the System

Now let's examine a particular major scale and see how this system works: the E-major scale, for instance. In answer to the first question (does the scale have sharps or flats?), the scale would have sharps, because its root is a natural note other than F. In answer to the second question (how many sharps or flats are in the scale?), the scale will have *four*, because sharps go from left to right and E is the *fourth* scale from the left. Now, as to the third question (which sharps or flats are in the scale?), the answer will be the *first four* sharps: F, C, G, and D. We have already mentioned that all major scales have one and only one of every letter name, so the E-major scale should now be simple to construct. Just say the musical alphabet from E to E and add accidentals where appropriate. Thus, the E-major scale is E, F *sharp*, G *sharp*, A, B, C *sharp*, D *sharp*, and E.

Let's look at its flat counterpart, the E♭-major scale. In answer to the first question, it will be a flat scale because E♭ already has a flat in its name. This scale will have *three* flats, because in the acronym GDAEBF, E is the *third* from the right. Finally, in answer to the question, "which sharps or flats are in the scale?", they will be the first three from the right in the acronym FCGDAEB, or B♭, E♭, and A♭. Thus, the E♭-major scale is E *flat*, F, G, A *flat*, B *flat*, C, D, and back to E *flat*.

While this learning technique may initially seem more complicated than the 2-2-1 system of half-steps outlined earlier, after a couple of days of practice you will find that you can easily construct any of the major scales from memory.

By the way, there are two major scales (in addition to the C-major scale that has no sharps or flats) that are not covered by this system. These scales, however, are infrequently used and very easy to remember. They are C♯, in which all the notes are sharped (C♯, D♯, E♯, F♯, G♯, A♯, B♯, C♯) and C♭, in which all the notes are flatted (C♭, D♭, E♭, F♭, G♭, A♭, B♭, C♭).

Using the "three questions" system, derive the following major scales: G, D♭, F, B♭, A, F♯, D, A♭, and B. Check each scale using the 2-2-1 system to make sure it is correct, and if there are any discrepancies, check your answers against those in the appendix. If this is your first exposure to major scales, I strongly recommend spending several days making sure you have them memorized before going on to the rest of the material in this book, as virtually everything we discuss will relate back to them in some way.

Keys and Key Signatures

How many times have you heard phrases such as: "This song is in the key of G"; "Let's try this song in the key of B♭"; or "The original record was in the key of D"? Those of you who are beginners in music theory may not be entirely clear as to exactly what the word "key" means. In terms of what we've already discussed in this chapter, we can loosely define a *key* as *the major scale on which most of the melody and chord progression of a song are based.* Thus, if a song is in the key of C, the majority of its melody notes will be taken from the C-major scale, and most of the chords used will be diatonic to (contained within the scale of) C major. To let us know what key a song is in, the writer will place a *key signature* at the beginning of the song, which tells us the number of sharps or flats the key contains. For example, this is the key signature of Van Morrison's "Have I Told You Lately" which was a major hit for Rod Stewart in 1993.

Notice that after the treble clef, the flats are written on the appropriate line and space for B and E. This tells us that the song is in the key of B♭ because, as we discussed earlier, the B♭-major scale has two flats: B and E. In addition to informing us of the key of the song, the key signature makes it easier to write out the melody, because once a note is sharped or flatted in the key signature, all notes bearing the same letter (in this case B and E) are automatically sharped or flatted throughout the song. Should the composer want to use B or E natural, the natural sign (♮) would be used to cancel out the sharp or flat.

The sharps or flats in a key signature are written in a particular order: the same order as the answer to the third question in the method for deriving major scales we discussed earlier. Thus, when there are two flats in the key signature, the B♭ is written first, followed by the E♭, as illustrated above. Similarly, when a song has two sharps in the key signature, they are written F♯ and then C♯. Three sharps are written in the order F♯, C♯, G♯, and so on. By convention, these sharps and flats are written in specific places on the staff. Illustrated below are the key signatures for C♯ (all seven sharps) and C♭ (all seven flats).

To get a picture of what the key signature of any key looks like, simply cover the sharps or flats not wanted on the diagram above. For example, placing a piece of paper over the A, D, G, C and F flats will reveal the key signature of two flats to be exactly the same as in the example from "Have I Told You Lately" illustrated above.

A final note regarding key signatures: although they are always used when writing out lead sheets or melodies for a song, I don't recommend using them when doing the exercises on chord progressions presented in Chapters 7–12 and 17. It will help eliminate misunderstanding to use the appropriate accidentals on each chord, and reserve the use of key signatures for melodies and lead sheets.

Intervals

In most music theory classes, a lot of time is spent generally on the subject of intervals. Based on my experience as a songwriter, however, I've found that much of this material is not necessary for understanding intervals as they specifically apply to pop melody and harmony, so I'm going to give you a sort of "crash course" in the essentials instead.

Studying intervals is less confusing when you realize that an interval is nothing more than *a way of expressing the distance between two notes.* In other words, saying that two notes are a major third or a perfect fourth apart is no different from saying the bass player and the guitarist in a band are standing two or three feet from one another on stage. Intervals are nothing more than convenient ways of expressing how close or far one note is from another. They are especially useful when examining chord extensions (ninths, elevenths, and thirteenths), as we will do in Chapter 12, or when analyzing relationships between pitches in a melody, as we will see in Chapter 13.

A key fact in making the study of intervals easy to understand is that *the names of intervals are always derived from the major scale of the lower note.* Thus, if we are describing the interval (distance) from F on the first space of the treble staff to C on the third space of the treble staff, we express that distance in terms of the F-major scale, because F is the lower of the two notes.

Types of Intervals

Intervals are of five specific types: perfect, major, minor, diminished, and augmented. The distance from a note to the fourth or fifth note in its major scale or to itself an octave higher is known as a *perfect interval.* Thus the distance from C to F is called a perfect fourth, from C to G a perfect fifth, and from C to C a perfect octave. The distance between a note and the second, third, sixth, or seventh note in its major scale is known as a *major interval.* Thus the distance from C to D is called a major second, from C to E a major third, C to A a major sixth, and C to B a major seventh. These major and perfect intervals are illustrated below.

Major	Major	Perfect	Perfect	Major	Major	Perfect
2nd	3rd	4th	5th	6th	7th	Octave

The minor and diminished intervals represent major and perfect intervals in which the top note is lowered a half-step. *A major interval lowered a half-step is called a minor interval, while a perfect interval lowered a half-step is called a diminished interval.* Thus, because the distance between C and E is a major third, the distance between C and E *flat* is known as a *minor third.* Similarly, because the distance between C and G is a *perfect* fifth, the distance from C to G *flat* is called a *diminished* fifth. *Augmented intervals* are either major or perfect intervals where the top note is raised a half-step. Thus, because the distance from C to F is a perfect fourth, the distance from C to F *sharp* is an *augmented* fourth. Similarly, because the distance between C and A is a major sixth, the distance between C and A *sharp* is an augmented sixth.

Finally, to determine intervals of notes more than an octave apart, we merely add seven to what the interval would be if the notes were in the same octave. In the example below, to determine the distance between C on the ledger line below the treble staff and E♭ on the top space of the treble staff, we simply determine the distance between C and the E♭ an octave lower, which would be a minor third. We then add seven to it so that the new interval is called a minor tenth.

It's important to remember once again that intervals are always determined by the *major scale* of the *lower* note, so the distance between D and F♯ is a major third rather than an augmented third, because F is sharped in the key of D. Similarly, the distance between F and B♭ is a perfect fourth rather than a diminished fourth, because B is flatted in the key of F.

Learning to Hear Intervals

Becoming familiar with these intervals is extremely important in writing melodies, because each one has a characteristic sound that can be used to create a particular melodic effect. You can learn to identify the sound of different intervals by thinking of songs that feature them in prominent places. That way, when we discuss them in the chapters on melody writing, you will understand them aurally as well as theoretically.

The interval between the first two words of the chorus of the Fine Young Cannibals' "She Drives Me Crazy," for example, is a major third, while Larry Henley and Jeff Silbar's "The Wind Beneath My Wings" (which was both a country hit for Gary Morris and a pop hit for Bette Midler) begins on a major sixth ("It must . . ."). Leonard Bernstein's musical *West Side Story* provides us with an abundance of memorable melodies that begin with specific intervals, such as "Tonight" (perfect fourth), "Maria" (augmented fourth), and "Somewhere" (minor seventh).

> Play or sing and identify the following intervals, remembering to base your identification on the major scale of the *lower* note. Check your results against those in the appendix.

Wrap-Up

In this chapter we have explored how the pitches we discussed in Chapter 4 combine to form major scales and intervals, from which the melodies of songs are created. In the next chapter we're going to complete our inquiry into the theoretical basis for hit songwriting by looking at the chords derived from those scales.

6

Chords:
The Featured
Fourteen

As we demonstrated in Chapter 1, harmony or chord progression is an essential part of a song's musical makeup. Indeed, many successful songwriters regularly begin their writing process by creating an interesting chord progression as a harmonic framework before adding lyrics or melody. Let's look at the fourteen types of chords from which these progressions are formed. With the exception of extensions and alterations such as ninths, elevenths, and thirteenths (which will be discussed at length in Chapter 12), virtually every part of the harmonic accompaniment of every song that has ever been recorded is derived from these fourteen chord types. In this chapter we'll be looking at how they are constructed so that we can explore how they work together to form chord progressions in subsequent chapters.

Triads

The first four chords we're going to examine each contain three notes and hence are called *triads*. The most common of these is the

46

major triad, which is formed from the *first, third, and fifth notes in the major scale of the root.* Thus, for example, a D-major triad is composed of D (the first note in the D-major scale), F$\sharp$ (the third note in the D-major scale), and A (the fifth note in the D-major scale). This chord is both the simplest and the most common of all chords used in contemporary music. When a songwriter or musician speaks of a "D chord" or an "F chord," the full theoretical name of the chord to which he or she is referring is a D-major triad or an F-major triad.

The second chord we're going to look at, which is also the second most frequently used, is the *minor triad.* It is formed from the first, *lowered* third, and fifth notes in the major scale of the root. (*Note:* Whenever I use the terms "lowered" or "raised" in explaining chord construction, I mean raised or lowered by a half-step.) Therefore, the notes in a D-minor triad (Dm) are D (the first note in the D-major scale), F (the third note in the D-major scale lowered a half-step), and A (the fifth note in the D-major scale). Incidentally, when lowering the third note in the scale to form a minor chord, it is important to always maintain the same letter name. Thus, the lowered third of an F-minor (Fm) chord would be an A$\flat$ rather than a G$\sharp$. This practice also holds true for lowering or raising scale notes to form the other chords discussed in this chapter and may necessitate the use of double sharps ($\times$) or double flats ($\flat\flat$).

The remaining two triads you need to be aware of are far less common than either the major or minor. They are the *augmented* triad, built from the first, third, and *raised* fifth notes in the major scale of the root, and the *diminished* triad, built from the first, *lowered* third, and *lowered* fifth notes in the major scale of the root. The notes in a D augmented triad (generally written D+) are D, F sharp, and A *sharp*, and the notes in a D diminished triad (generally written D°) are D, F natural, and A *flat*. Illustrated below are the four triads we have just discussed built on the root D.

D	Dm	Daug	Ddim
Major Triad	Minor Triad	Augmented Triad	Diminished Triad

As I've mentioned several times, the ability to connect what you *study* with what you *hear* is the key to successfully applying this knowledge to your songwriting. As I present the various chords in this chapter and as we discuss their application in chord progression in future chapters, be certain you are constantly connecting your theoretical understanding of them to their sound by playing them on your keyboard or guitar, or listening to the examples of their use in the hit songs I refer to.

Triads in Action

Major triads have a brighter and happier quality than their minor counterparts. Think of the opening measures of two hits from Garth Brooks' multiplatinum *No Fences* album: "Unanswered Prayers" (major chord) and "The Thunder Rolls" (minor chord). Or listen to the first four measures of Bob Dylan's "Knockin' On Heaven's Door" (recorded by both the writer and by Guns N' Roses), illustrated below.

As you play or listen to this excerpt, focus on the difference in sound between the A *minor* chord at the end of the first phrase ("Mama, take this badge off of me") and the C *major* chord at the end of the second ("I can't use it anymore").

Examples of the augmented and diminished triads are far less prevalent. The augmented triad has an unusual, almost eerie feeling and is used often in movie sound tracks to create tension. It is the second chord in both Eddie Money's "Baby Hold On" (co-written with Jimmy Lyon) and Michael Masser and Linda Creed's "The Greatest Love of All" (recorded by Whitney Houston as well as George Benson). The diminished triad, which has a classical sound and was quite popular in the music of the eighteenth and nineteenth centuries, is rarely used in today's pop, rock, or country. It is, however, the building block upon which the *diminished seventh,* which we'll discuss later in this chapter, is constructed.

The Three Most Common Seventh Chords

The other chords that contemporary songwriters use frequently are four-note chords known as *sevenths* because the interval between the highest and lowest notes in each chord is always a seventh. The most common of these is the *dominant seventh* chord, which consists of a major triad (1–3–5) plus the *lowered seventh* note in the major scale of the root. The notes in a D seventh chord (written D7), for example, would be D, $F\sharp$, and A (the D-major triad) plus C *natural* (because C sharp is the seventh note in the D-major scale). This chord, because of its tendency to need to resolve (discussed more thoroughly in Chapters 7 and 8), is often used as the last chord in a verse to propel us into the chorus. Songs that use the dominant seventh in this way include Bonnie Raitt's 1994 hit "Love Sneakin' Up on You" (written by Tom Snow and Jimmy Scott) and Randy Travis's "Forever and Ever, Amen," which won the 1987 Country Song of the Year Grammy for co-writers Don Schlitz and Paul Overstreet. Dominant seventh chords are also the primary chord upon which traditional blues progressions are built, and often a song such as Huey Lewis's "The Heart of Rock and Roll" (co-written with Johnny Colla) or Patty Loveless' "You Will" (by Randy Sharp, Pam Rose, and Mary Ann Kennedy) will begin with a dominant seventh chord and sustain it over several measures to give the song a more "bluesy" feel.

The other chord we can look at as an extension of the major triad is the *major seventh* chord. It is formed by adding the unaltered seventh note in the major scale of the root to the major triad. Thus, the notes in a D-major seventh chord (written Dmaj7) will be D, $F\sharp$, A, and C *sharp*. This chord has a very distinctive sound, which can most readily be brought to mind by recalling the introduction to Chicago's "Color My World," which consists of an arpeggiated (played note by note) major seventh.

The third seventh chord that's extremely common in today's music is the *minor seventh* chord, formed from the *minor* triad and the *lowered* seventh note in the major scale of the root. Thus, the notes in a D-minor seventh (written Dm7) are D, F, A, and C *natural.* This chord has a sound similar to that of a minor triad, but fuller and richer. Compare the sound of the minor triad which is the first chord in the verse of George Strait's "I Cross My Heart" (written by Steve Dorff and Eric Kaz) to the minor seventh chord that begins the fifth measure ("From here on after . . ."), and you will hear the difference in quality between these chords.

These three chords—the dominant seventh, major seventh, and minor seventh—are by far the most important seventh chords in contemporary popular music. In fact, each of them individually is used more than all the rest of the chords we're going to discuss in this chapter *combined.*

Other Important Seventh Chords

The next chord we're going to look at is an unusual one whose use is almost exclusively limited to a particular progression: the *minor major seventh.* It's formed by adding the regular seventh note in the major scale of the root to a minor triad. Thus, the notes in D-minor major seventh (abbreviated Dm maj7) are D, F (the lowered third), A, and C *sharp* (the regular seventh). This chord is generally found in the progression going from Dm to Dm maj7 to Dm7, illustrated below.

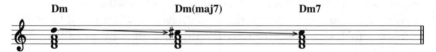

Notice that the bottom three notes of each of these chords form a Dm triad, and the top notes form a descending chromatic (half-step) line going from D to C♯ to C. If you play this progression on your keyboard or guitar, you'll immediately recognize its sound. The Oscar-winning French composer Michel Legrand is especially fond of this sequence of chords, having used it in the opening measures of such classics as "The Summer Knows" (theme from *Summer of '42*), "What Are You Doing the Rest of Your Life?," and Barbra Streisand's "The Way He Makes Me Feel" (from her movie *Yentl*), all with lyrics by Alan and Marilyn Bergman. The progression is not limited to more traditional motion-picture music, however. It has also been used quite successfully by rock and roll writers such as George Harrison (on the "don't want to leave her now" section of his hit "Something") and Jimmy Page and Robert Plant (in the opening measures of their Led Zeppelin classic, "Stairway to Heaven").

The next two chords we're going to look at are variations on the dominant seventh chord. The first, the *augmented seventh,* is formed by adding the lowered seventh note in the major scale of the root to the augmented triad. Thus, the notes in a D augmented seventh (written D+7) will be D, F♯, A♯, and C. This is a very powerful chord that combines the dramatic quality of the augmented triad with the dominant seventh's need to resolve. Two examples are the second chord of the introduction of Stevie Wonder's "You Are the Sunshine of My Life" (the ascending Fender Rhodes instrumental line), and the last chord of the chorus of Steely Dan's "Josie," accompanying the lyric "with her eyes on fire."

The dominant seventh sus [suspended] *4 chord,* the use of which will be discussed extensively in Chapter 8, is a dominant seventh chord with the *fourth* note in the major scale of the root replacing the third. Thus, the notes in a D seventh sus 4 (written D7sus4) will be D, G (the fourth note in the D-major scale), A, and C. This chord, popularized in the late '60s and early '70s through the Carole King/James Taylor sound, has less of a dramatic pull to resolution than the dominant seventh, because of the absence of the tritone (diminished fifth interval), which is formed between the third and lowered seventh of that chord. To appreciate this difference, listen to the chord that sustains through the first three bars of the verse of Hugh Prestwood's "The Song Remembers When," which was a hit for Trisha Yearwood in 1993, then try singing the melody of those measures over a plain dominant seventh chord.

Chords Derived from the Diminished Triad

Next, let's look at the two chords that are built on the diminished triad. The first of these, the *minor seventh flat 5* (classically called the "half diminished") consists of a diminished triad and the lowered seventh note in the major scale of the root. The notes in Dm7♭5, then, will be D, F, A *flat,* and C. Perhaps an easier way to think of this chord is as a minor seventh with a lowered fifth. It is more commonly found in songs in minor key, such as the Lennon/McCartney collaboration "Because" (from the Beatles' *Abbey Road* album) and Don Henley's "New York Minute" (co-written with Danny Kortchmar and Jai Winding).

The *diminished seventh* is a rather unusual-sounding chord that consists of a diminished triad plus the *doubly lowered* (lowered a *whole* step) seventh note in the major scale of the root. Thus, the notes in D diminished seventh are D, F, A♭, and C *flat* or B. An interesting fact about this chord is that it consists entirely of minor third intervals, the interval between each note in the chord and the next being a minor third. Because a minor third consists of three half-steps and there are twelve half-steps in an octave, the diminished seventh chord divides the octave into four equal parts. Because of this, the notes in the D diminished seventh, F diminished seventh, A♭ diminished seventh, and B (or C♭) diminished seventh are *exactly the same*. If you listen to the second measure of both the introduction and the verse of Garth Brooks' "Friends in Low Places" (by Dewayne Blackwell and Bud Lee) on the *No Fences* album, you'll hear the distinctive sound of this chord.

Sixth Chords

The last two chords we're going to look at were used more extensively in the music of the '30s, '40s, and early '50s than they are today, but nevertheless should still be a part of the modern composer's repertoire. They are the *major sixth* and *minor sixth*. The major sixth, as the name implies, consists of a major triad plus the sixth note in the major scale of the root (a D-major sixth chord is spelled D, F♯, A, and B and written D6). The minor sixth consists of the *minor* triad plus the sixth note in the major scale of the root (D, F, A, and B are the notes in a Dm6). Although these chords are not nearly as popular as they were thirty or forty years ago, it's still important that you become familiar with how they are constructed (and, more important, with how they *sound*) so that you can freely use them from time to time when you feel they are appropriate.

Wrap-Up

I have illustrated below these "featured fourteen" chords in the key of D. Play them on your instrument and be certain you are familiar with both the sound and the theoretical construction of each one before going on with the rest of the work in this book. In the next two parts we'll be looking at how these chords combine within a given key to form chord progressions.

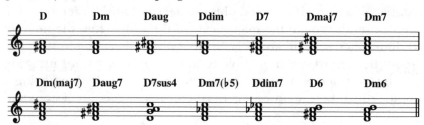

Write the "featured fourteen" chords built on the roots A, B♭, B, E♭, E, F, and G as I have done in the key of D above. Compare your results with those in the appendix and then play or listen to each one until you are familiar with its sound as well as how to construct it.

Part Three

Pop Harmony
The Building Blocks

7

Diatonic Chords

Now that we've completed our study (or for some of you, our review) of the basics of theory, notes and note values, scales, and chords, we're going to look at how these elements are combined to create hit songs. Generally, songs are written in one key and utilize specific chords that occur most frequently in that key. (We'll discuss songs written in more than one key in the chapter on modulation, Chapter 11.) To understand the way chord progressions are used, we must become familiar with the chord families found in each key.

Diatonic Chords

In Chapter 6, you wrote out all the chords built on C, such as C dominant 7, C minor, etc. However, a C-minor chord is not commonly found in the *key* of C major, but a D-minor chord is, because D minor is *diatonic* to that key and C minor is not. What do we mean by diatonic? Classically, it is defined as "contained within a given scale." For example, the note E is diatonic to the G-major scale because E is the sixth note in that scale. However, the note G is *not* diatonic to the

57

E-major scale because G *sharp* is the third note in that scale, not G. The most basic chords in the chord family in any given key, then, are the diatonic chords that are *composed entirely of notes from within the major scale of that key.* Thus, the diatonic chords in the key of C are made up of all natural notes, because the C-major scale contains no sharps or flats.

Diatonic chords are the most important building blocks in contemporary hit songs. Many songs, ranging from country hits such as Garth Brooks' "The Dance" (written by Tony Arata) to rockers such as Pat Benatar's "Hit Me with Your Best Shot" (written by Eddie Schwartz) to classics such as "Up on the Roof" and "The Tracks of My Tears," consist entirely of diatonic chords. Even writers such as Billy Joel and David Foster, who frequently use nondiatonic harmony, still base their work on the diatonic structures, and more than half the chords in their songs are diatonic.

Let's look at exactly what these diatonic chords are. First, we'll write out a C-major scale in one octave.

Now, let's build four-note chords on each note of the scale using only notes that are diatonic to the key of C, i.e., contained within the C-major scale.

Next, let's analyze these chords and see what they are. The first chord C–E–G–B is a C-major seventh. The next, D–F–A–C, is a D-minor seventh. The rest of the chords are E-minor seventh (E–G–B–D), F-major seventh (F–A–C–E), G dominant seventh (G–B–D–F), A-minor seventh (A–C–E–G), and B-minor seventh flat five (B–D–F–A).

The triads formed from the first three notes of these sevenths are also important diatonic chords. Throughout this book, whatever we say about seventh chords will also be true for the triads they contain, unless otherwise noted. Here are the diatonic *triads* in C major.

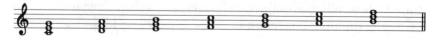

As you can see, they are C–E–G (C major), D–F–A (D minor), E–G–B (E minor), F–A–C (F major), G–B–D (G major), A–C–E (A minor), and B–D–F (B diminished).

Roman Numerals

We're going to use a system called *Roman numeral notation* to analyze songs. These Roman numerals are derived from the major scale of the root of the key. Thus, in the key of C, any chord beginning on C will be called a I chord, any chord beginning on D will be called a II chord, any chord built on E♭ will be called a flat III chord (because E is the natural third in the key of C), etc. Here is the formula for the Roman numerals of the diatonic seventh chords in the key of C.

The formula for the diatonic triads, then, will be I, IIm, IIIm, IV, V, VIm, VIIdim.

> To make certain that you understand what we've discussed so far, write out on a sheet of staff paper the diatonic triads in the keys of A, B♭, B, D♭, D, and E, and the diatonic sevenths in E♭, F, G♭, F, and A♭. Use the same procedure as above: (1) write out the major scale (remembering to use accidentals and not key signatures), (2) build up three- and four-part chords on each degree of the scale using only diatonic notes that are contained within that major scale, and (3) analyze your chords both by name and Roman numeral and check your results against those in the appendix.

Your results should be the same in all keys. The diatonic structures will come out to be Imaj7 (or I), IIm7 (IIm), IIIm7 (IIIm), IVmaj7 (IV), V7 (V), VIm7 (VIm), and VIIm7♭5 (VIIdim). If you commit this formula to memory, you can easily identify any diatonic chord in any key. For example, if you wanted to know what a III chord in the key of E was, you would find the third note in the E-major scale (G♯) and, by using the formula, would know that a III chord is a G♯ *minor triad* or G♯ *minor seventh.* Try this process with several chords before going on to the rest of the chapter, as a thorough grasp of it will make your journey onward much easier.

Diatonic Chords at Work

Now we're going to examine how these chords are used in songwriting. Let's look at the first four measures of "Almost Over You" (co-written by Jennifer Kimball and Cindy Richards), which Sheena Easton carried to the top of the pop charts in 1985.

You'll notice that a lot of harmonic movement occurs in these first four measures. In fact, five different chords are used, all of them diatonic. Because the song is in the key of $A\flat$, as the key signature reveals, the $A\flat$ in the first measure is a I chord. In the next measure we find a C minor (IIIm), followed in the third measure by $D\flat$ (IV) and $B\flat$ minor 7 (IIm7). In the fourth measure, the IIm7 is repeated, followed by a V7 ($E\flat7$). With the exception of the VIm and VIIm7$\flat$5 chords, *all* the diatonic chords are used within the first four measures of this song.

Harmonic Functions

To enable you to work with these chords more effectively, I'm now going to introduce a method of categorizing them by *harmonic function.* The diatonic chords are grouped into three harmonic functions, the quality of each chord determining its function. Before going into further detail, I need to clarify two things.

First, those of you who have studied classical music should be forewarned that the terms I use to describe the harmonic functions are not defined exactly as *The Harvard Dictionary of Music* would define them. Obviously, those of you who have never had formal music training won't have any problem with this usage.

Second, because it is difficult to describe and define harmonic functions, the best way to understand them is by analyzing songs and hearing them in action. An analogy I often use with my students is this: A person who was blind has just been given sight and you have the task of describing the color yellow to her. You might say it is warm and bright, but by that definition she could confuse it with white or tan, both of which are warm and bright. You would ultimately realize that the best way to describe the color yellow is to point out things that are yellow until the person finally "gets" what yellow is. It is the same with harmonic functions. Although my explanations will be helpful in getting started, analyzing songs and *hearing* which chords fall within which harmonic functions is the only way to fully understand them.

Tonic, Dominant, and Subdominant Functions

The three harmonic functions into which diatonic chords are categorized are: *tonic*, which will be abbreviated "(T)," *dominant*, which will be abbreviated "(D)," and *subdominant*, which will be abbreviated "(SD)." Tonic can be "defined" (remember our analogy with the color yellow) as being "at rest." There are, however, varying degrees of being at rest. For example, if you're running and slow down to walk for several minutes before running again, you're at rest compared to when you were moving more rapidly. "At rest" doesn't necessarily mean totally stopped.

Dominant can be defined as "needing to resolve," but again there are different degrees of need. Suppose it's 3:00 p.m. and you haven't had lunch yet. You could say that you "need" to eat, but your need is probably very different from that of someone who hasn't eaten in several days. So needing to resolve is also a relative term and can indicate different degrees of need.

The third harmonic function, subdominant, can be defined as "moving along" or "in between" tonic and dominant. While a subdominant chord does not have the need to resolve that a dominant chord does, it is not as "at rest" as a tonic is. Again, you will appreciate these harmonic functions more fully once you've started listening to their *sound* in the context of familiar songs.

The I, IV, II, and V Chords

Each diatonic chord has a particular harmonic function, which remains constant no matter what the key or harmonic context. To illustrate this, let's look at the beginning of the chorus of "The Power of Love" (by Derouge, Mende, Applegate, and Rush), which was originally recorded by Air Supply in the 80's and later became a number 1 hit for Celine Dion in 1994.

As you listen to this excerpt, pay close attention to the tonality of each chord. Because the song is in the key of A♭, the first chord, A♭ major, is a diatonic I chord. Its harmonic function is *tonic* and you can hear its quality of being "at rest".

The next two chords, D♭-major and B♭-minor (the IV and II minor chords) are both *subdominant* in function. Notice their "moving along" quality in comparison to that of the tonic chord that precedes them.

The last chord in this example, the E♭-major or V chord, is *dominant* in function. As you play or listen to it, notice how this chord wants to pull your ear back to the tonic I and has a stronger "need" to resolve than any of the others.

These opening measures illustrate a basic tendency of music: to go from tonic (at rest), to subdominant (moving along), to dominant (needing to resolve), and then back to tonic. In this way, music imitates life. We begin at peace (tonic), then move through life creating situations (subdominant), until we reach a crossroad where we need to make a decision one way or the other (dominant). When we do decide, our life is temporarily at rest (tonic) until the cycle begins again. Although songwriters will frequently combine chords with these functions in a different order to produce a particular effect, the basic tendency of harmony to move from tonic to subdominant to dominant to tonic is one of the cornerstones of music writing.

The III, VI, and VII Chords

The VIIm7♭5 chord, like the V7 chord, is *dominant* in function but, unlike the V7 chord, it is seldom if ever heard in today's music. Its triadic version, the VII diminished, is used frequently in classical music and can occasionally be found in songs where a classical feeling is desired, but examples of the chord in contemporary pop, country, or R&B are few and far between. The other two diatonic chords, the IIIm7 and VIm7 are, however, quite common. To examine their functions, let's look at another classic hit, Michael Masser's "The Greatest Love of All" (lyrics by Linda Creed), which climbed to the Top 40 in a version by George Benson and later reached number 1 in a recording by Whitney Houston. Here are the first measures of the chorus of that song.

As you can tell by the key signature, the song is written in the key of A. Notice that in the third measure the B-minor 7 and the E7 chords are the same IIm (subdominant) and V7 (dominant) chords we encountered in "The Power of Love." However, instead of resolving to the tonic I chord, Masser resolves them to two other chords, a IIIm7 (C#m7) and VIm7 (F#m7), both of which are *tonic* in function. As you will recall, when we used the analogy of walking after running, we defined tonic as "at rest" but not necessarily totally stopped. Notice that although the IIIm7 and VIm7 chords do not have as static a quality as the I chord, they are more "at rest" than the IIm7 subdominant and V7 dominant chords. They are often, in fact, used in place of the I chord, another important technique of writing, which we're now going to examine.

Substitution by Function

Imagine that you are getting dressed to go out with some friends and decide it would be appropriate to wear jeans. You reach into your closet only to discover that your favorite jeans have a hole in them and can't be worn. What do you do? Obviously, you wouldn't substitute a pair of dress slacks or a bathing suit. If jeans are the appropriate garb, you'd put on another pair of jeans or some other casual pants. Similarly if you're writing a song and hear a IV chord as appropriate but decide for any number of reasons to use a different chord (such as having already used a large number of IV chords and wanting to create contrast), you could substitute a IIm7, which is also a member of the subdominant family. Substituting one chord for another with the same harmonic function is called *substitution by func-*

tion. An excellent example of this occurs in the fourth measure of the chorus of Dan Hill and Barry Mann's "Sometimes When We Touch."

This song is in the key of D, and the chorus begins with a I chord (T) going to a IV (SD) followed by a V (D) chord. Because of the subdominant–dominant–tonic tendency discussed above, we next expect a return to the I chord on the words "too much," but instead Mann cleverly substitutes a IIIm chord. Because it is also tonic, it completes the tonic–subdominant–dominant–tonic cycle as a I chord would, yet sounds different enough to add variety. Try playing the passage going to a I (D-major) chord rather than a IIIm and listen to the difference.

Harmonic Analysis

Throughout this book, we will employ a particular system of harmonic analysis as we examine how chord progressions are used. To illustrate this system, let's return to the first four measures of "Almost Over You." First, we write the chord symbols within the staff and the key followed by a colon above the staff.

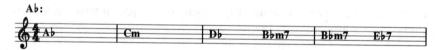

Next, we write the Roman numerals above each chord symbol and the harmonic functions above the Roman numerals so our example looks like this:

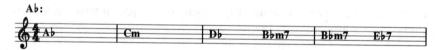

Before harmonically analyzing a song, it's important to become familiar with its sound either by playing the chord progression through several times while singing the lyrics or by listening to the recorded version. Then analyze it in the manner illustrated above.

Finally, play it through once more and see if you can make a connection between your theoretical understanding of the music and your aural experience.

We are now going to analyze Garth Brooks' number 1 hit "The Dance" (by Tony Arata), which we referred to at the beginning of this chapter. If you are not familiar with "The Dance," it would be a good idea to buy a copy of the recording and/or sheet music before proceeding with the analysis. Below is a chart of the chord changes for the verse and chorus of the song. Copy them onto a sheet of staff paper and analyze them in the way we have described, writing the key followed by a colon at the beginning, and the appropriate Roman numeral and harmonic function above each chord symbol. If you have trouble determining the key by ear, listen for a major chord that sounds tonic. This will be the I chord, because that is the only chord that is both tonic in function and major.

After you have completed your harmonic analysis of the song, compare it with the correct analysis in the appendix and then play it through again and listen closely. How do the subdominant, dominant, and tonic chords interact with one another? Do you notice any examples of substitution by function? In what interesting or distinctive ways are chord progressions used?

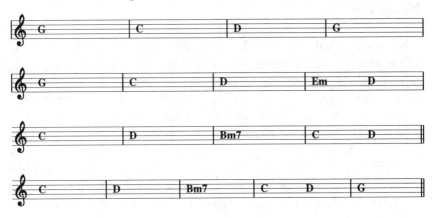

ANALYSIS

The song begins with a short piano introduction in the key of E minor not shown on this chart that sets the emotional stage for the bittersweet lyric that follows (remember our discussion of prosody in Chapter 3). We then hear the tonic–subdominant–dominant–tonic (I–IV–V–I) progression we've already discussed. The next four bars repeat that progression, except that the final I chord is replaced by a VI minor (Em): the technique of substitution by function we also referred to earlier.

The chorus, in contrast to the verse, begins on a IV subdominant chord (C major), which is then followed by a V dominant (D major). This time, however, a different substitution by function is used. Instead of resolving to a I tonic chord (G) or a VI minor (Em), the writer goes to a Bm7 (III minor 7), the same substitution used in both "The Greatest Love of All" and "Sometimes When We Touch." After this progression is repeated, we then hear IV and V within one measure (note the change in harmonic rhythm), finally coming back home to the I chord at the end of the chorus, which emotionally enhances what Garth Brooks himself refers to as the "anthem-like" quality of the song.

SUGGESTED ASSIGNMENT

Write an original song using only diatonic structures. Keep the harmonic functions in mind as you are writing and use substitution by function in at least one place. When the song is completed, write out a chord chart with analysis as we did for "The Dance."

Wrap-Up

It is extremely valuable to take songs you admire and analyze them harmonically. As the Grammy-winning songwriter Jay Graydon puts it, "The best way for writers to study their craft is to take tunes off records verbatim, note for note, look at them and figure out what's happening. Professionals do that all the time. Say you want to write a tune for Boz Scaggs for example, you're going to listen to what Boz did the last time or you're going to try to think of something that he would fit into that someone else has done. And if *you* have a hit like "After the Love Is Gone" [which Jay co-wrote with David Foster and Bill Champlin], the next time around you're borrowing from yourself."

Although melodies and lyrics are strictly copyrighted and cannot be "borrowed," chord progressions are not protected in the same way. Should an interesting series or use of chords strike your fancy, you are free to let it inspire your own harmonic ideas in any way you choose. As we continue in subsequent chapters to expand our knowledge of the different chords that are available, you will be able to completely analyze more and more of today's hits. As a stepping-stone to creating your own original music, there is no substitute for understanding how other writers have successfully used chord progressions.

8

Flat VII and Sus 4

Now that we've thoroughly explored the diatonic structures, we're going to add two new chords to our vocabulary that can contribute additional flavor and spice to your writing. These chords, the flat seven ($\flat$VII) and the suspended fourth (V7sus4), occur in many contemporary hits from the mellow pop sound of Neil Diamond and James Taylor to the varied musical styles of diverse artists such as Van Halen, Patty Loveless, and Tori Amos. As you become familiar with them, you'll see them cropping up frequently when you analyze your favorite songs, and you'll be able to integrate them into your own writing as well.

The V7sus4

Let's begin by examining the two dominant chords in the key of C, the V7 and the seldom-used VIIm7$\flat$5, to determine what makes them dominant.

67

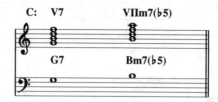

Notice that both these chords contain the notes B and F, the seventh and the third of the key, and that, in fact, no other diatonic chords in the key contain both those notes. These two notes form an interval comprising three whole steps, which is known as a *tritone*. This tritone is perhaps the most unstable interval, and because of its cliff-hanging effect, it was referred to in classical music as "the devil's interval." Play it on your keyboard or guitar and notice how it "wants" to resolve. Usually, the resolution is by half-step, the B moving up to C (the root of the key) and the F moving down to E (the third of the key), which creates a tonic I chord, completing the dominant-to-tonic motion. In the case of the V7 (G7), the bass note G moving down a fifth (or up a fourth) to C is also an essential part of the resolution.

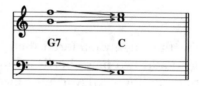

Songwriters, particularly in recent times, have often opted to use a dominant chord that has a more subtle resolution: the V7sus4. As we discussed in Chapter 6, the V7sus4 chord is a dominant seventh chord containing the fourth instead of the third note of the major scale of the root. Thus, in the key of C, the V7sus4 chord would be G7sus4.

When resolving this chord to a I (C) tonic chord, the G-to-C bass resolution and the F-to-E resolution are still present, but the tritone is missing, because the B of G7 has been replaced by a C. Play

G7sus4 to C and listen to the difference between its sound and that of G7 to C. Although the V7sus4 is still dominant (has a "need" to resolve), it is "less" dominant than the V, much as the IIIm and VIm chords are "less" tonic than the I chord.

> Before we discuss how the V7sus4 chord is used in contemporary hit music, it's important that you become familiar with its sound as well as the way it's constructed. Take out a piece of staff paper and write the V7sus4 chord in all twelve keys (G7sus4 in the key of C, A♭7sus4 in the key of D♭, A7sus4 in the key of D, etc.). Compare your results with those in the appendix and then play the V7sus4 chord in each key until you can readily identify its sound.

Let's look at an example that vividly illustrates the difference between the V7sus4 chord and the V7 chord. Below are the opening bars of Neil Diamond's "Hello Again" (co-written with Alan Lindgren) from his 1980 remake of the movie *The Jazz Singer*.

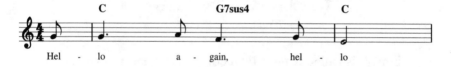

Because the song is in the key of C, the opening chord, C major, is a I major triad, tonic in function. The next chord, the G7sus4, is the V7sus4 we've been discussing. As you play or listen to the example, notice the sound of the G7sus4 (V7sus4) as it resolves to the I (C) chord. Now play the progression along with the melody, but substitute a G7 (V7) for the G7sus4. You can hear how "straight" and predictable the resolution of the G7 is, and how subtle the effect of the G7sus4 chord is in comparison.

In classical music, where the V7sus4 chord first originated, it was almost invariably resolved to the V or V7 before moving to the I or tonic chord. Today, however, we're free either to resolve it directly to the I chord (as Neil Diamond does in "Hello Again") or to emulate classical composers by first resolving it to the V7, as writers Karen Taylor-Good and Burton Collins do throughout their 1994 country hit, "How Can I Help You Say Goodbye?", recorded by Patty Loveless.

Although V7sus4 can be found in all styles, from country to jazz to R&B, it has a distinctively "pop" sound. You would be hard pressed to find a song by a "pop" composer such as Neil Diamond, Burt Bacharach, or Michael Bolton that does not make use of it or one of its substitutes at some point (see Chapter 11 for a discussion of chords that function as substitutes for the V7sus4). It is also sometimes used in its triadic form, Vsus4, particularly in rock and roll tunes such as Van Halen's "Jump."

The ♭VII

We are now going to explore our first nondiatonic chords, the ♭VII and the ♭VII major seventh (♭VIImaj7). First, let's start with an examination of the VIIm7♭5 chord (in the key of F for variety), which, as we said in Chapter 7, is seldom if ever found in pop music. If we lower the root of this Em7♭5 (VIIm7♭5) chord a half-step, however, we get a chord that is quite common, the ♭VIImaj7 (in this case, E♭maj7).

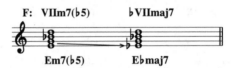

E♭maj7 is called a *flat* VII major 7 because E natural is the seventh note in the F-major scale. This chord is more commonly used in its triadic form (an E♭-major triad in the key of F), which would be called simply ♭VII.

> Before proceeding further, take out a piece of staff paper and write out the ♭VII and ♭VIImaj7 chords in all twelve keys, i.e. B♭–D–F and B♭–D–F–A in the key of C, B–D#–F# and B–D#–F#–A# in the key of C#, etc. Be sure to write out the name of each chord as well. Check your results against those in the appendix and play the ♭VII and ♭VIImaj7 chords resolving to the I chord in each key on your keyboard or guitar.

Here is an example of the ♭VII chord as it is used at the end of one of the Beatles's most popular songs, "Hey Jude."

Because the song is in the key of F, the E♭ chord in the second measure is the ♭VII chord. Play or listen to this progression and pay particular attention to the sound of the E♭. Although it clearly has its own distinctive flavor, it is grouped along with IIm7 and IV in the subdominant family. Play it again and substitute first a subdominant chord such as the Gm7 (IIm7), then a tonic chord such as Am7 (IIIm7), and finally a dominant chord (C7 or C7sus4) for the E♭. You can hear that, although the E♭ chord is unique, it sounds subdominant in that it has neither the resting quality of the tonic chord nor the immediate need to resolve of the dominant chord.

The Two Uses of the ♭VII

The ♭VII and ♭VIImaj7 chords are generally used in two different ways. First, they can be "surprise" chords after an extended series of diatonic chords. An excellent example of this occurs in Elton John's "Can You Feel the Love Tonight" (lyric by Tim Rice), which won the Academy Award for Best Song in 1995 for its use in the motion picture *The Lion King.*

The song is written in the key of B♭, and bars one through three consist of a repeated IV–I (E♭–B♭) progression, followed by the IIm7 (Cm7) and V(F) chords in the fourth measure. Bars five through seven are a repetition of bars one through three, with the exception of the substitution by function of a VI minor (Gm) for I at the end of the seventh measure. In the eighth measure, however, where we expect a return to the IIm, Elton completely surprises us by inserting a ♭VII (A♭) chord. Although it has the same function as the IIm7 it replaces, it sounds quite striking because it is the first nondiatonic chord we have heard. This use of a ♭VII as a surprise at the end of a verse or chorus is a technique that has been used successfully for many years. Examples range from standards like Jimmy Webb's "By the Time I Get to Phoenix" to modern alternative songs like Tori Amos' "Silent All These Years."

The second common use of ♭VII/♭VIImaj7 is as an integral part of the song. In this case, it is usually introduced close to the beginning of the tune and thus becomes basic to the overall feeling. A good example occurs in Patti Smyth's 1992 hit, "Sometimes Love Just Ain't Enough" (co-written with Glen Burtnik). Both the introduction and the first two phrases of that song are written over a I–VIm7–♭VII–I progression. Because it is introduced so early and repeated several times, the "exotic" sound of the ♭VII is no longer a surprise as in "Can You Feel the Love Tonight" or "Silent All These Years," but rather becomes an integral part of the tonality.

The most common use of the $\flat$VII in this way is the I–$\flat$VII–IV–I progression that we studied earlier in the Beatles' "Hey Jude." Other tunes where we find that progression range from folk-influenced ballads such as James Taylor's "Country Road" and "Fire and Rain" to rock hits such as Richard Marx's "Don't Mean Nothing" and Collective Soul's "Shine."

Now that we have looked at how some of today's top writers have used the V7sus4 and $\flat$VII chords, it's your turn to analyze part of a song that features both of them: the verse of Giorgio Moroder's 1983 theme from the movie *Flashdance*, "What A Feeling," with lyrics by Keith Forsey and Irene Cara. Utilize the system of analysis we learned in the last chapter: write the key with a colon followed by the Roman numeral analysis and then put the harmonic function of each chord above its Roman numeral. Remember to play the verse through before analyzing it. Check your analysis against that in the appendix and then play it through again, listening for the interplay of chord progression, melody, and lyrics (refer to the original recording or sheet music if you're not familiar with the tune). What can you learn from this song that can be applied to your own writing?

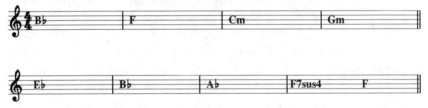

ANALYSIS

Notice how the first six measures of the song are composed solely of diatonic chords, the B$\flat$ (I), F (V), Cm (IIm), Gm (VIm), and E$\flat$ (IV). Because Moroder is an accomplished classical composer and film scorer, the song has a very classical feeling, which is enhanced by chords that are triadic and by a melody in which the first note played against each chord alternates between the third and the fifth of the chord (D is the third of B$\flat$, C is the fifth of F, E$\flat$ is the third of Cm, etc.). Thus, a peaceful harmonic atmosphere is created that is suddenly disrupted by the surprise interjection of the $\flat$VII (A$\flat$) in the seventh measure, a very nonclassical pop chord. In the second verse, Moroder brings the drums into the arrangement along with the $\flat$VII, clearly signaling to us that this is a hard-driving dance tune and not the classical ballad that we might have mistaken it for initially. The A$\flat$ chord in each verse is followed by an F7sus4 chord (V7sus4), which Moroder, in keeping with the classical feeling, first resolves to the V chord (F) before returning to the I.

SUGGESTED ASSIGNMENT

Write an original song consisting primarily of diatonic chords that uses at least one V7sus4 and one $\flat$VII or $\flat$VIImaj7. Experiment both with resolving the V7sus4 to V and then to I and with resolving it directly to I. Also notice whether you are using the $\flat$VII chord as an integral part of the song or as a "surprise" chord.

Wrap-Up

The V7sus4 and $\flat$VII chords we have explored in this chapter are but two of several sophisticated harmonic devices that can add color and a contemporary sound to your writing. I'll introduce many others later, but you can already create memorable songs as Elton John, Richard Marx, and Giorgio Moroder have done using only what we have studied so far. The more you analyze the songs of writers you admire and absorb the subtle nuances in their writing, the more skilled your own compositions will become. In-depth analyses, such as the ones we have performed here on "Can You Feel the Love Tonight" and "What A Feeling," are an invaluable aid in discovering what really makes a hit song work. I strongly encourage you to do as much of this kind of analysis as possible.

9

Secondary Dominants

In this chapter, we're going to learn about another series of chords that can add variety and richness to your songwriting. They're called *secondary dominants* and are used in all styles of music, from the simplest Hank Williams country to the most sophisticated contemporary R&B/pop by writers such as Boz Scaggs and the team of Jimmy Jam and Terry Lewis. Once you become aware of them, you will notice how often they crop up in songs you analyze. They are easy to master, can add spice to a basic diatonic progression, and are a valuable addition to your bag of songwriting tricks. Let's examine how they are constructed and used.

The Dominant–Target Chord Relationship

In Chapter 7, we learned that the dominant seventh chord in every key is built on the fifth note in the major scale. G7, therefore, will be the dominant of C, and A7 will be the dominant of D. Play a D chord followed by an A7 on your piano or guitar and you'll notice that you are left feeling "up in the air." Now play the A7 again, resolving it

74

back to the D chord, and you'll notice that the ear "wants" to hear this dominant A7-to-D resolution. We call the chord to which a dominant chord resolves its *target* chord. In this case, D is the target chord of A7. Here are some further examples.

Dominant Chord	Target Chord
F7 ⟶	B♭
B7 ⟶	E
D7 ⟶	G

Because F7 is the V or dominant chord in B♭, B♭ is the target chord of F7. Similarly, E is the target chord of B7 because B is the fifth in the key of E, and G is the target chord of D7 because D is the fifth in the key of G.

Although we haven't yet delved into minor keys, it's important to our study of secondary dominants to be aware that this same dominant-target relationship also occurs there. In that case, the V7 chord would resolve to a I *minor* target chord. (See Chapter 17 for a more extensive discussion of minor-key harmony.) Thus, the target chord of A7 can also be D minor, because A7 is the V7 in that key as well. This holds true in all minor keys, as illustrated below.

Dominant Chord	Target Chord
F7 ⟶	B♭m
B7 ⟶	Em
D7 ⟶	Gm

To summarize, the dominant chord (A7) is always built on the fifth note of the major scale of the root of the target chord (D or Dm). Conversely, the target chord (D or Dm) is always built on the *fourth* note of the major scale of the root of the dominant chord (A7). Now, let's look at the relationship of a *secondary* dominant to its target chord.

What Is a Secondary Dominant?

The way I usually explain secondary dominants and target chords in my classes is to compare them with a sister and brother. For example, I have a sister named Connie. You could describe her through her relationship to me, saying that she is the sister of a songwriter or the sister of the author of this book. Should I win a Grammy next year, you could then say that she is the sister of a Grammy winner.

Whatever I am, Connie is the sister of that. Carrying this analogy one step further, because I am a member of the National Academy of Songwriters, you could say that my sister also has a particular relationship to the National Academy of Songwriters; although she has never written a song in her life, she is the sister of a member. She has a closer relationship to the Academy than other nonmembers, but a relationship that is less direct than mine. My relationship is primary: I am a member. Her relationship is secondary: she is the sister of a member.

Returning to music, let's compare this to the relationship between an A7 chord and the key of C. In Chapter 7 we learned that the diatonic VI chord in the key of C is an A *minor* seventh chord. Therefore, an A7 chord does not have a *primary* diatonic relationship to the key of C. It does, however, have a relationship to one of its target chords, D minor, which is the diatonic II minor chord in that key. You might say that an A7 chord has a relationship to the key of C *only* through the D-minor chord, much as my sister has a relationship to the National Academy of Songwriters only through me. Because an A7 chord is a V7 of the diatonic IIm in the key of C, it is called the V7 of II and is considered a *secondary dominant* in that key.

A secondary dominant can be defined as a *dominant chord whose target chord is diatonic to the key*. Because there are seven diatonic chords, you might expect that there would be seven secondary dominants, but that is not the case. The V7 of I is not a secondary dominant because it is the *primary* dominant of the key, much as if my sister were a songwriter and a member of the National Academy of Songwriters herself. The V7 of VII chord is only a theoretical possibility because the target chord, the VII minor 7♭5, is seldom if ever used, as discussed in Chapter 7.

There are, then, five frequently used secondary dominants in any given key: the V7 of II, the V7 of III, the V7 of IV, the V7 of V and the V7 of VI. Here are the secondary dominants of the key of C.

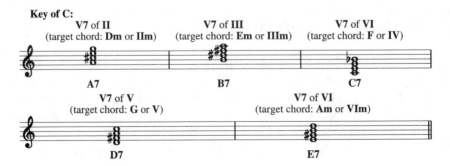

Before proceeding, write out the secondary dominants in the keys of A, B♭, D, E♭, F, and G, following the model of the example above. Be sure to include the notes of the chord on the staff, the name of the chord, and the name of its target chord. Check your results against those in the appendix. If you made any mistakes, go back and see whether they were caused by lack of understanding of the secondary dominant–target chord relationship and, if so, reread the first part of this chapter before going on.

How Secondary Dominants Are Used

We're now going to look at how songwriters incorporate secondary dominants into their writing. Basically, these chords make us anticipate the arrival of their target chords, just as my sister's arrival at the National Academy of Songwriters office would make people there assume that I would soon be arriving, because her only relationship to the organization is through me.

If you play a I–IV–V–I progression in the key of C (C–F–G–C) followed by an A7 chord, you'll notice that the ear "wants" to hear a resolution to the target D-minor chord. We'll illustrate this tendency using a short melody in the key of G. Play or sing this example.

Now, let's harmonize this melody with simple diatonic chords, employing a I (G-major chord) in the first measure, a VI minor (E-minor chord) in the second measure, and a IV (C-major chord) in the third measure. (Reread Chapter 7 if you're not clear on the analysis of these chords.) Play or sing the melody again with the accompanying chords shown.

We've created an interesting harmonized melody, but by using secondary dominants, we have the possibility of making it even more interesting.

Let's insert a B7 (V7 of VI) chord on the last two beats of the first measure, creating the expectation of its target E-minor (VI minor) chord that follows on the first beat of the second measure. In the same vein, let's insert a G7 (V7 of IV) chord on the last two beats of the second measure, making our ears "want" to hear its target C-major (IV) chord that follows in the third measure. (I have altered F♯ to F natural in the melody of the second measure to harmonize with the G7 chord.) Now play or sing our example with this new harmonic accompaniment.

After including these secondary dominants, the tune becomes clearly recognizable as Boz Scaggs's "We're All Alone," which was originally recorded by the composer and later became a top-10 hit for Rita Coolidge.

> Here's the verse of Billy Joel's "The Longest Time," which we discussed briefly in Chapter 1. Analyze it as you did the examples in Chapters 7 and 8, writing the Roman numeral of the chord above the chord symbol, and the harmonic function (tonic, dominant, or subdominant) above the Roman numeral. Remember, secondary dominants are written as "V7 of II" and are dominant in function. Check your results against those in the appendix, and see if you fully comprehend the basic use and resolution of secondary dominants before reading the rest of the chapter.

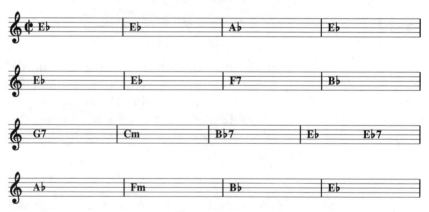

The Three Types of Secondary Dominants

Three types of chords can be used as secondary dominants. The most common is the dominant seventh, such as the B7 on the third and fourth beats of the first measure of "We're All Alone." Major triads can also be secondary dominants because of the rule discussed in Chapter 7: whatever we say about seventh chords is also applicable to the triads they contain. The only exception is the V7 of IV, which cannot be a major triad because it would then be merely a I chord (in the key of G, for example, G7 is the V7 of IV and a G-major triad is the I). Finally, secondary dominants (like primary dominants) can be V7sus4 chords (see Chapter 8). Play "We're All Alone" and substitute a B-major triad or a B7sus4 chord for the B7 chord and listen to the difference. Actually, when Boz Scaggs originally wrote the song, he used a B7sus4 on the third beat of the measure, resolving it to a B7 on the fourth beat.

Variations on Secondary Dominants

Sometimes writers will cleverly exploit our expectation that a secondary dominant will be followed by its target chord and surprise us with an alternative. Diane Warren, for example, resolves a V7 of II chord to a IV at the beginning of the chorus of her 1990 Taylor Dayne number 1 hit "Love Will Lead You Back." This is an example of substitution by function, because we expect a subdominant chord to follow the V7 of II; the writer gives us a subdominant chord, but not the one we anticipate. This device is quite common and can be used to offset the predictability of secondary dominant–target chord resolution without jarring the ears.

From time to time, however, a writer will resolve a secondary dominant to a chord that has no relation whatsoever to the target chord. We find this effect in the chorus of the 1986 Grammy-winning Song of the Year, "That's What Friends Are For" (music by Burt Bacharach and lyrics by Carole Bayer Sager). Analyze the three measures of the chorus illustrated below, and check your analysis against the appendix. (Note: The last chord, the $Abm6/Cb$, is a IV minor 6, a nondiatonic chord whose function will be discussed in Chapter 18.) We're in the key of Eb, and we begin with the fifth measure of the chorus.

The C7 chord in the second measure is the V7 of IIm (F minor). However, instead of following it with the F-minor chord as expected or with its related subdominant IV as Diane Warren did, Bacharach surprises us with an Ab-minor sixth. This adds a fresh and unusual flavor to the last syllable of the lyric "forevermore."

Another technique contemporary writers use is to precede a secondary dominant with the II minor 7 of its target chord (or the II minor 7♭5 if the target chord is minor), creating what could be called a *secondary subdominant*. An excellent example of this occurs at the beginning of the chorus of Boyz II Men's "On Bended Knee" (written by Jimmy Jam and Terry Lewis), which topped the charts for 6 weeks in 1994–5.

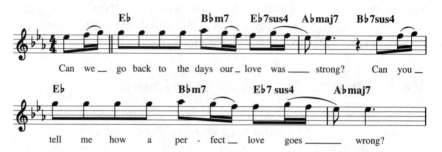

The V7 of IV–to–IV progression from the first to second and third to fourth measures of this chorus is the same one Boz Scaggs uses in "We're All Alone," with one exception: The A♭-major 7 (IV) chords are preceded by their secondary subdominant B♭-minor 7ths as well as their secondary dominant E♭7sus4s, enhancing the effect of the "temporary modulation" to the key of the target chord that occurs whenever a secondary dominant is used. David Foster is especially fond of this technique, having incorporated it into many of his hits, including De Barge's "Who's Holding Donna Now?" (co-written with Randy Goodrum and Jay Graydon) and Chaka Kahn's "Through the Fire" (co-written with Tom Keane and Cynthia Weil). Kenny Loggins also makes use of it twice in the first four measures of his classic "Whenever I Call You Friend" (co-written with Melissa Manchester).

SUGGESTED ASSIGNMENT

Write an original song using at least two different secondary dominants. Analyze the song harmonically and pay particular attention to how you resolve the secondary dominant chords. Also, try inserting some secondary dominants into songs you have already completed and see if you like the effect.

Wrap-Up

As we have seen, contemporary writers use secondary dominants in many inventive ways to add variety to their songs. Although we have delved into some of the more unusual resolutions, about 80 percent of all secondary dominants resolve to their target chords, while another 10 to 15 percent resolve to chords with the same function as their target chords. Remember, these are just rough percentages rather than specific guidelines to follow in your own writing. When using a secondary dominant, as with any chord progression, the bottom line is always, "Does it sound good and enhance the melody and lyric?"

Part Four

Modern Harmonic Techniques

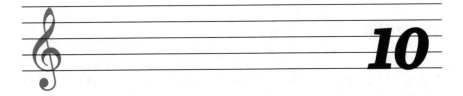

10

Inversions

The chords we discussed in Part III have formed the cornerstone of successful songwriting from as far back as George Gershwin and Cole Porter to the current Top 40. They include the seven diatonic chords, the flat VII and V7sus4, and the five secondary dominants. Along with the chords used in or borrowed from minor keys discussed in Chapters 17 and 18, they account for more than 99 percent of the harmonic basis of popular music in the twentieth century. There are literally tens of thousands of songs recorded and released every year, not to mention hundreds of thousands of songs written during the same time period, which are built entirely on these chords.

How is it possible, then, that composers have been able to create such an endless variety of harmonic colors with such a limited palette to choose from? The answer lies in the techniques of enhancing these chords that we're going to be discussing in this section: inversions, modulation, and extensions. Learning to use them can make the difference in your writing between adequate harmonic accompaniment and creating sounds comparable to the exciting and innovative songs written by consistently successful contemporary hitmakers such as Bruce Springsteen, Bryan Adams, Clint Black, and U2.

85

Inversions

In classical music the term "inversion" generally refers to a chord played in other than "root position," that is, other than with the root on the bottom, the third above, and the fifth above that. The most common inversions are the 6/3 chord (which features the third in the bass) and the 6/4 chord (which features the fifth in the bass). For our purposes, however, we're going to use a different definition that, while not "classically" correct, will encompass the wide variety of harmonic variations used today. We will define an inversion as *a chord with any note other than the root in the bass.*

In contemporary music, these chords are sometimes referred to as "slash chords." This is not because they are favored by the lead guitarist of Guns N' Roses, but rather because we generally use a slash (/) symbol to notate them. The name of the chord is placed to the left of the slash and the bass note is written to the right. Thus, a G chord with a B in the bass would be written as G/B. Similarly, a G chord with an F♯ in the bass or an A in the bass would be written as G/F♯ or G/A.

In this chapter, we're going to explore the three categories into which more than 90 percent of the inversions used in today's music fall. It is important to bear in mind, however, that inversions don't *necessarily* have to belong to one of these categories, and that as a songwriter you are free to use any inversion at any time just because it sounds good to you. However, I strongly recommend becoming familiar with the three more traditional usages before experimenting with possibilities that fall outside of them, as it will give you a more solid foundation upon which to build.

Pedal Point

Those of you who followed rock and roll in the mid-'80s can probably recall the opening sections of the verses of two of that era's biggest hits, Michael Sembello's "Maniac" and Rick Springfield's "Affair of the Heart." The beginnings of both songs were marked by an ominous feeling of building tension similar to that of the chorus of Steve Perry's "Oh Sherrie" or the section leading into the chorus of Night Ranger's "Sister Christian," two other rock hits of the same era. In all of these cases, the tension was created by a harmonic device called *pedal point.* Simply stated, pedal point consists of *repeating a series of chords over a single bass note.* Let's look at another example: the opening measures of the verse of Dan Hill and Barry Mann's "Sometimes When We Touch," whose chorus we examined in chapter 7.

The best way to appreciate the difference made by pedal point is to play this example first with and then without it. When you play it without the pedal point, play both the G chord in the second measure and the A in the third measure with the root (G or A) in the bass. Although that version still sounds perfectly fine, notice the prosody with the lyric "and I choke on my reply" that results from the additional tension created by the pedal point.

There is no inherent limit to the amount of time or number of chords for which pedal point may be used. The opening measures of the chorus of U2's "Mysterious Ways" and the prechorus of Pearl Jam's 1992 hit "Jeremy" (written by singer Eddie Vedder and bassist Jeff Ament) are among the many contemporary examples of an extended use of pedal point.

Sometimes a pedal point is held only briefly, often for as few as two chords. This occurs twice in the first five measures of Lionel Richie's "Endless Love" (which hit number 1 on the charts in 1981 as a duet by Richie and Diana Ross and number 2 in 1994 as a duet by Luther Vandross and Mariah Carey). The two pedal points Richie uses in that passage are those most frequently found in popular music: the *dominant pedal,* where the common bass note is the fifth note in the scale of the key, and the *tonic pedal*, where the common bass note is the root of the key.

Pedal points are also sometimes used as part of "instrumental hooks," distinctive musical phrases and/or chord progressions that are an integral part of the arrangement of songs (see Chapter 20). Often these instrumental hooks also function as part of the harmonic accompaniment of the songs themselves. Examples of songs with instrumental hooks that use pedal points include Billy Joel's "My Life" and Christopher Cross' first hit "Ride Like the Wind."

Inversions Used to Create Bass Motion

Michael Bolton is one of the most commercially successful artist/songwriters of the '90s. Before his success as a vocalist, however, he was known for his skills as a songwriter, having composed, among others, Laura Branigan's 1983 Top 20 hit "How Am I Supposed to Live Without You" (co-written with Doug James), which later became a number 1 hit for Michael himself in 1990. One of the techniques he employs consistently is the use of inversions to create a particular type of bass motion. Let's look at an example in the opening measures of the verse of "How Am I Supposed to Live Without You."

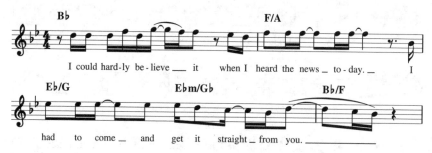

See how the chord tones Bolton uses in the bass form a continuous descending line from B♭ to F. Play this example through both with these inversions and with the normal roots in the bass of the chords, and listen to the difference in the sound.

Types of Bass Motion

Inversions can be used to create two types of bass motion: scalewise (following the major scale of the key), as in the first five measures of

"How Am I Supposed To Live Without You" or chromatic (by half-step), as in the fifth through seventh measures. Furthermore, these bass lines can be either ascending or descending. In terms of prosody, descending lines such as the one above, or at the beginning of the Carole King/Gerry Goffin classic "Natural Woman" (as recorded by Aretha Franklin and others), tend to be pensive, reflective, or even melancholy in nature. Notice that, although nothing in Bolton's lyric tells us what type of "news" the singer "heard today," the music itself makes it clear that it is not good news. That message is conveyed, in large part, by use of the descending bass line.

Conversely, ascending bass lines such as the one in the chorus of "Up Where We Belong," mentioned in Chapter 3, tend to evoke more positive, hopeful feelings. I used this technique at the beginning of the chorus of my song "Bridges of Love" (co-written with Stephen Fiske), which Jose Feliciano recorded for an international television special.

As you play this example, notice the uplifting quality of the ascending chromatic bass line created by the use of inversions in the third measure. Now play it again with the root in the bass of the D and F# chords, and listen to the difference. Notice also that, like pedal points, the use of inversions for bass motion can be limited to one chord as in "Up Where We Belong" or can be played through a series of chords as in "How Am I Supposed To Live Without You" or "Bridges of Love."

The Substitute Sus (Suspended Fourth)

While there are literally hundreds of different ways in which inversions can be used to create pedal point and scalewise or chromatic bass motion, there are only two possible examples in any given key that fit into our third category for the use of inversions. Yet these two possibilities alone are used as frequently as all the possibilities combined in either of the other two categories. The "inversions" used in this category (remembering our definition of inversion as any chord with a note other than the root in the bass) are substitutions for the V7sus4 chord discussed in Chapter 8; hence I refer to them as the *substitute sus* chords. Let's investigate the structure of these chords by looking at the V7sus4 chord in the key of C.

I've written the notes of the chord in the treble clef in an order different from the usual one, but note that they are the same (G, C, D, and F) as if I had written them with the root as the lowest note.

At this point, to fully understand the substitute sus, we need to skip ahead a little bit and discuss very briefly the concept of the ninth, which we'll explore in greater detail in Chapter 12. What you need to know for the moment is that the ninth of a G7sus4 chord is the second degree of the G-major scale (A), so by substituting an A for the G in the treble clef, we arrive at a chord that is actually a G9sus4.

If you play both of these chords, the V7sus4 and the V9sus4, and resolve them to the tonic I chord (C major), you can hear that they are both dominant in function and that their sound is quite similar. If you look more closely at this V9sus4 chord, however, you will notice that the notes in the treble clef, D, F, A, and C, form a Dm7 chord. This chord, then, is most commonly written as Dm7/G, but actually *sounds* like a G9sus4 (or G7sus4) chord.

The second variation of this substitute sus chord is produced when we omit the fifth of the G9sus4. This leaves us with F, A, and C (an F-major triad) in the treble clef over G in the bass clef, written F/G. Thus the two possible substitute sus chords in any given key are the IIm7 with the V in the bass (Dm7/G in the key of C) and the IV major triad with the V in the bass (F/G in the key of C). Let's listen to an example of how these chords are used from the opening of Tom Snow's "Somewhere Down the Road" (lyrics by Cynthia Weil), which was a hit for Barry Manilow in 1982.

C   C/E   F   Em7

We had the right — love   at   the   wrong —   time,

Dm7   Dm7/G   Dm7/C   C

Guess I al - ways knew— in - side—   I would-n't have— you for a long— time

The Dm7/G chord in the fourth measure is an example of the substitute sus we've been examining. Now play the example with a G7sus4 chord in place of the Dm7/G. You'll hear that the IIm7/V chord, while it sounds very similar, is a richer and more interesting substitution, which is why it is consistently favored by many of today's most successful songwriters. Notice also that in these first five bars Snow also uses inversions for bass motion (the C/E in the first measure) and as a pedal point (the Dm7/C resolving to C in the fifth measure).

The IV chord with V in the bass has also been a part of our musical tradition for many years. It's used as the primary dominant chord immediately before and throughout the chorus of a number of well-known songs, ranging from country hits such as Wynonna's "She Is His Only Need" (written by Dave Loggins) to contemporary R&B classics such as Boyz II Men's "End Of The Road" (by Babyface, L. A. Reid, and Daryl Simmons).

We're now going to analyze a song that makes use of all three categories of inversions. Although Anne Murray has had several number I country hits, we're going to look at the song that was her only number I pop hit, Randy Goodrum's "You Needed Me." As before, copy the chart onto a piece of staff paper and play the chord progression through on your keyboard or guitar while you sing or hum the melody (if you are not familiar with it, it would be a good idea to buy the record or sheet music). Then write the Roman numeral analysis above the chord changes and the harmonic function above the Roman numeral analysis. (Note: the C#dim7 chord in the fifteenth measure is dominant in function.) Also notate the particular use of inversion, using the abbreviation "PP" for pedal point, "M-C" for chromatic bass motion, "M-S" for scalewise bass motion, and "SS" for substitute sus. Compare your results with the analysis in the appendix, and once your analysis is correct, listen closely to the effect that these inversions have upon the music. An excellent way to do this is to play the song through both with and without the inversions and compare the results. Do this before going on to the next section.

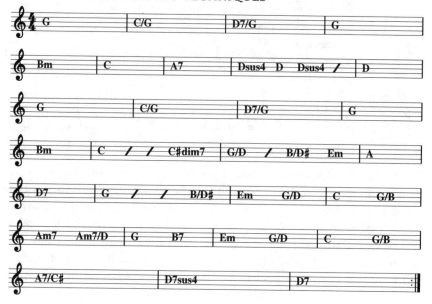

ANALYSIS

Notice that the chord most strongly impacted by the pedal point in the first four measures is the B minor that follows. I often ask my students jokingly, "Why is using a pedal point like beating your head against the wall?" The answer, of course, is the old cliché, "Because it feels so good when you stop." The pedal point, which creates dramatic tension, profoundly affects the chord that follows it because the tension finally releases at that point.

Starting in the fourteenth measure, a series of chords with an ascending chromatic bass line is used to accompany the lyrics "You put me high upon a pedestal, so high that I could almost see eternity." When playing this passage without inversions, notice the absence of the strong prosody of the ascending bass line accompanying that lyric. Then, in the bridge section, the song shifts to a descending scalewise bass line, which culminates in the substitute sus, Am7/D, in the twenty-second measure. This bass line is then reintroduced, only instead of continuing down to A as it did the first time, it reverses direction abruptly, going to A7/C# with the lyric "I finally found someone who really cares." Playing "You Needed Me" both with and without inversions is one of the most vivid illustrations possible of the power of these chords.

SUGGESTED ASSIGNMENT

Write a song that uses at least four inversions, with at least one example each of pedal point, chromatic motion, scalewise motion, and the substitute sus. Play your song through both with and without these inversions and notice the difference in the texture of the sound.

Wrap-Up

As you can see, inversions are extremely valuable tools for enhancing and deepening the sound of the building blocks of pop harmony we studied in Part III. They're found in all idioms of music, from R&B to contemporary country to hard-driving rock and roll. While some songs use them outside of the three basic categories we have described in this chapter, more than 90 percent of inversions in today's music involve either pedal points, substitute suses, or chromatic or scalewise bass motion. By continuing to analyze songs that contain inversions and starting to experiment with them yourself, you'll gradually become more and more creative in integrating them into your own writing.

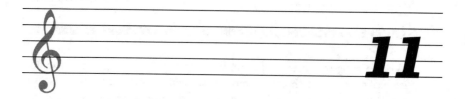

Modulation

In Chapter 10 we examined how hit songwriters enhance the quality of the chords available within a given key by using inversions. In this chapter, we're going to expand our harmonic vocabulary even further by looking at a way to increase the *number* of chords at our disposal when writing a song. This method enables us not only to double or triple, but to actually multiply the number of available chords by eleven! This becomes possible when we realize that, although there are a limited number of chords in any given key, *we may move from one key to another within the duration of a song.* This changing of keys, or *modulation*, makes possible a large number of harmonic (as well as melodic) variations that do not exist when a piece remains in the key in which it begins.

Modulation serves several other important functions as well. For example, let's say you're working on a new song and have written a great verse. The next day you write an absolutely terrific chorus, but after putting them together you notice that the melodic range of the chorus falls below that of the verse, lessening the dramatic impact. Rewriting one or both of the melodies is an alternative, but it is also possible to *modulate* into a higher key in the chorus so that the relationship between the melody and harmony remains intact, but the overall range is higher than that of the verse.

Another reason to use modulation is to create contrast such as we discussed in Chapter 3. This particular use of modulation is most commonly found in the bridge section of a song (which is included primarily to provide such contrast), especially in songs with an A-A-B-A form where the bridge is the only variation from the verse. Billy Joel, who as we mentioned in Chapter 2 is particularly fond of this form, uses modulating bridges in songs such as "She's Got a Way," "Leave A Tender Moment Alone," and "New York State of Mind." Later in this chapter we'll be looking at how Bryan Adams and Eric Clapton used modulating bridges in their hits, "(Everything I Do) I Do It for You" and "Tears in Heaven."

As you work through this chapter, listen closely to songs you hear on the radio and see if you can learn to aurally identify the modulations we're going to be discussing. Most of today's successful composers, from writer/artists such as Kenny Loggins and Sting to successful "outside" composers such as Barry Mann and Diane Warren, use it extensively in their writing. Once you've mastered the *two types of modulation* and the *two ways to modulate*, you'll find that this device will have a great impact on your own writing as well.

The Two Types Of Modulation

We're now going to look at the two types of modulation that are available to us. Both are used extensively, yet each has its own distinct sound. Occasionally you will even find both of them within the same song. Next, we'll be looking at the two *ways* of modulating, either of which can be used with either *type* of modulation.

The Arranger's Modulation

First we're going to examine what is called an *arranger's modulation*. It consists of repeating the harmonic, melodic, and lyric material of a song in a different key, usually up a half-step or whole step, and generally at the end of a tune. It is used frequently on the final chorus of a verse/chorus song (especially when it is repeated two or more times) to create a dramatic, uplifting effect and to provide contrast, as in Whitney Houston's 1992 record-breaking hit version of

Dolly Parton's "I Will Always Love You." Songwriters often refer to it as the "Manilow Modulation," because Barry Manilow, who dominated the pop and adult contemporary charts in the late '70s and early '80s with more than twenty Top 10 hits, took extensive advantage of it. Listen to the endings of recordings, such as "Even Now" (by Manilow and Marty Panzer), "Looks Like We Made It" (by Manilow and Will Jennings), "Ready to Take A Chance Again" (by Fox & Gimbel), and "I Made It Through the Rain" (by Kenny/Manilow/Shepherd/Feldman/Sussman), to get a sense of the sound of this modulation. We call it an *arranger's modulation* because it is a part of the arrangement rather than the way a song is written; that is, it can be added or deleted at the discretion of whoever is arranging the song for a recording.

To appreciate the effect of the arranger's modulation, take any verse/chorus song you have written (or any verse/chorus song on the charts that you like) and play it through, repeating the chorus a half-step or a whole step higher at the end. If you perform this experiment with several songs, you'll notice that virtually any song may be played with an arranger's modulation at the end. Similarly, any song that has been recorded *with* an arranger's modulation may be performed without that modulation, and the basic melodic, harmonic, and lyric content will remain unchanged.

Variations of the Arranger's Modulation

Because it has been used for so many years, this device has a tendency to sound predictable. However, finding unusual variations of the arranger's modulation is limited only by the writer/arranger's creativity. An interesting one occurs in Berlin's Oscar-winning "Take My Breath Away" (music by Giorgio Moroder, lyrics by Tom Whitlock), an A-A-B-A song where the final A section is played in the key of B, a *full minor third* above the first two verses and the bridge, which are in A♭. A somewhat humorous variation occurs in Conway Twitty's 1980 number 1 country hit "I'd Love to Lay You Down" (words and music by Johnny MacRae), where the repeated choruses in the fade section are played *down* a whole step to create prosody with the song's title.

Although the songwriter may suggest it in his or her demo, the arranger's modulation will, for the most part, be added or deleted at the discretion of whoever is producing the final recording. Therefore it is not as important for us to examine in detail as is the second type of modulation, which we're going to look at next.

The Writer's Modulation

Unlike the arranger's modulation, the writer's modulation *is an essential part of the musical structure of a song.* It cannot be put in or taken out at the discretion of an arranger. An obvious example of this might be, for instance, to have the verse of a song written in one key and the chorus in another. A great number of successful songs have used this device, including Diane Warren's "Set the Night to Music," which was a top 10 duet in 1991 for Roberta Flack and Maxi Priest, and Survivor's 1985 hit "The Search Is Over" (by group members Frank Sullivan and Jim Peterik). However, the writer's modulation does not have to occur over as large a section of a song as an entire verse or chorus. Stevie Wonder's classic "You Are the Sunshine of My Life" uses a writer's modulation in the bridge that lasts for only two bars. After leading us through two full verses and eight measures of the bridge in the key of C, Wonder then includes the following phrase in the key of A.

And if I thought our love was end-ing

Notice that the phrase ends on an A-minor rather than an A-major chord, which is the beginning of its modulation *back* to the key of C. That is, in fact, one of the primary characteristics of writer's modulations: *they generally resolve back to the original key.* In "Set the Night to Music," for example, the opening verse is in the key of F, the chorus is in E, and the second verse returns to the key of F. The modulation in "The Search Is Over" provides an interesting variation of this return to the original key as it returns to E♭ in the *second half* of the chorus rather than waiting until the verse.

A common exception to this rule of returning to the original key happens frequently in songs where the bridge is the point of modulation. In these songs, the final chorus played after the bridge often comes back a half-step or whole step above the original key of the song, creating a sort of built-in arranger's modulation. For the most part, though, songs with writer's modulations return to their original key.

The possibilities and varieties of writer's and arranger's modulations are virtually endless. We're now going to take a more detailed look at how some of them work, with an eye toward how you can begin to incorporate them into your own writing.

Two Ways to Modulate

The Direct Modulation

The first method of modulating from one key to another is perhaps the simplest, the so-called *direct modulation,* where the song literally "jumps" from one key to another. The change of key in a song using this method usually sounds sudden and quite obvious to the ear. An example occurs in the prechorus of Earth, Wind & Fire's 1979 Grammy-winning R&B Song of the Year, "After the Love Is Gone" (co-written by David Foster, Jay Graydon, and Bill Champlin).

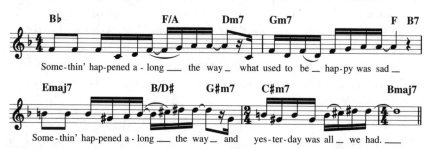

This section begins in the key of F on a IV (B♭) chord followed by a I chord with a third in the bass (F/A) and a VIm7 (Dm7) chord. In the next measure, the progression moves to a subdominant IIm7 (Gm7), finally resolving to the I tonic chord (F). In the third and fourth measures, the writers repeat the same chord progression and melody an augmented fourth higher in the key of B (with IV and I major seventh chords substituting for the triads). The actual point of modulation, however, occurs on the last beat of the *second* measure, where a B7 chord (the V7 of IV in B) is inserted to set up the Emaj7 that follows at the beginning of the next measure. As you listen to the example on the original recording or play it through on your instrument and sing the melody, you'll notice that this B7 chord has no relationship whatsoever to the key of B♭. When you first hear it, it signals an abrupt departure from that key, the sound characteristic of a direct modulation.

The Pivot Chord Modulation

A more subtle type of modulation available to us is known as a *pivot chord modulation.* This method of modulating, as the name implies, is based upon a chord that functions in both keys and *pivots* from one to the other. When you first hear the chord it sounds in the original key, but following the modulation it sounds like part of the new key. Pivot chords do not have to be diatonic to either key. They can be any one of the chords we have studied so far including the diatonic triads and sevenths, the flat VII and V7sus4, and the five secondary dominants, as well as any of the chords borrowed from the minor key we'll be discussing in Chapter 18.

The best way to fully understand the sound and effect of a pivot chord modulation is to listen to one. Let's examine the bridge of Bryan Adams' "(Everything I Do) I Do It For You" (co-written with Mutt Lange and Michael Kamen) which topped the charts for 7 weeks in 1991.

The verses preceding this bridge are written in the key of Db, and all the chords are completely diatonic to that key. When we first hear the B chord at the beginning of the bridge, therefore, it sounds like a bVII because our ears have become accustomed to the Db-major tonality and B (technically Cb) is the bVII in that key. After listening to the first four bars, however, it becomes clear that the B *also sounds* like a I chord in a I–IV–I–V progression. Therefore, it fits the definition of a *pivot* chord: "When you first hear the chord, it sounds in the original key, but following the modulation, it sounds like part of the new key."

Now play the bridge through again and pay attention to the second half. You'll notice that it returns to the original key of Db with a I–V–V7 of V–V progression, yet the transition back is so subtle that upon first listening you can hardly tell that there's been a modulation. That's because the writers again use a pivot chord: the F# (Gb) in the fourth measure that is *both* a V chord in B *and* a IV chord in D♭. Listen closely to this example several times, and you will begin to develop a sense of the way these pivot chords work.

An interesting variation of this more subtle style of changing keys is what I refer to as a "pivot" *melody* modulation. One of the most prolific and talented composers of the last three decades is Barry Mann, whose hits range from classics such as "On Broadway" and "You've Lost That Lovin' Feeling" to more recent recordings such as the 1987 Grammy winner for Song of the Year "Somewhere Out There" and Sergio Mendes's "Never Gonna Let You Go" which, between writer's and arranger's modulations, actually goes through eleven different keys! Mann uses this type of modulation going into the bridge of the Quincy Jones/James Ingram hit "Just Once" (with lyrics by his wife Cynthia Weil).

This excerpt begins on the last two measures of the chorus, which, like the rest of the song that precedes them, are in the key of C. The first chord is a IIm7 (Dm7), followed by a IV/V bass (the F/G substitute sus we spoke about in Chapter 10). As you play or listen to it, notice the way the melody interacts with this subdominant-to-dominant chord progression. We "want" to hear them resolve to a C-major chord with a C (the root) in the melody. Mann, in one sense, gives us the resolution that we desire (to a I major chord with a chord tone in the melody), but he resolves it instead to an A♭ chord where the C melody is the *third* rather than the root of the chord. Play these three bars with a C chord in place of the A♭ over the lyric "once," and you'll hear that this is the sound the ear expects. Now listen again with the A♭ chord in that spot and notice how, because Mann gives us the melody note we're anticipating (C) and keeps it as a chord tone, the modulation from the key of C to the key of A♭ sounds smooth and flawless.

We're now going to analyze a song that makes use of modulation: Eric Clapton's "Tears in Heaven" (lyric by Will Jennings), which won the Grammy for both Song and Record of the Year in 1992. Analyze the song as you have the examples in previous chapters. When the key changes, write the new key, followed by a colon at the point of the key change. For pivot chord modulations, show the function of the pivot chord in both keys. Play and sing the song through several times and listen carefully before completing your analysis, then compare it with the correct version in the appendix before continuing.

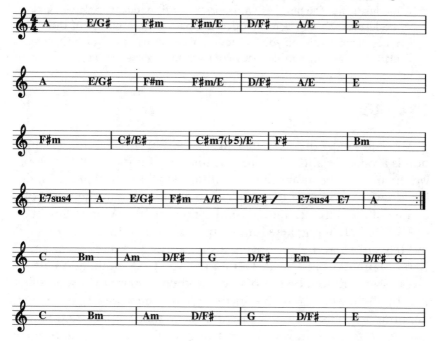

ANALYSIS

This song is written in an A-A-B-A form. The verses, although they use some nondiatonic harmony, are completely in the key of A. (The C#m7♭5 chord in the eleventh measure, by the way, is an example of the secondary subdominant we discussed in Chapter 9). At the C chord which begins the bridge section ("Time can bring you down ..."), the song moves abruptly to the key of G starting on a IV–IIIm–IIm–V–I progression. After repeating this progression in the fifth through seventh bars, Clapton goes to a D chord, then returns to the original key of A beginning on an E (V) chord. This modulation is more subtle than the one at the beginning of the bridge because the

D is a *pivot* chord: both V in the key of G and IV in the key of A. In fact, it is the exact same pivot chord that Bryan Adams used between the first and second sections of the bridge of "(Everything I Do) I Do It For You."

ASSIGNMENT

Write an original song that uses at least one writer's modulation. If you modulate into the new key with a pivot chord, modulate back with a direct modulation, or vice versa. Notice the difference in quality of these two types of modulation. If you feel adventurous, try using a pivot melody modulation or writing a piece that modulates through several keys.

Wrap-Up

As you can see by the examples we've cited in this chapter, modulation is a valuable and essential harmonic technique that we as songwriters need to be aware of as an option at all times. Whether we're just drawing two or three chords from another key in the space of a couple of measures as Stevie Wonder does in "You Are the Sunshine of My Life," changing keys for an entire section as Eric Clapton does in "Tears in Heaven," or moving a song through almost every key as Barry Mann does in "Never Gonna Let You Go," modulation always gives us an additional series of choices when our creativity seems limited by the options available in the key in which we began. As you continue to analyze more successful songs that employ modulation and begin to use it in your own writing, you'll see what a difference this technique can make.

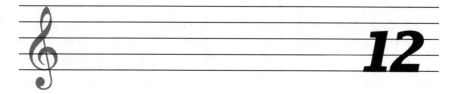

Extensions and Alterations

So far in Part IV we've explored the use of inversions, or different bass notes, and the use of modulations, or changes of key. Both of those techniques (with the exception of the substitute sus inversion) deal with ways of connecting groups of chords and sections of a song.

In this chapter, we're going to look at some methods for altering the tone colors of *individual* chords, making use of what we refer to as *extensions* and *alterations*. When applied to seventh chords, these extensions and alterations produce a more sophisticated sound characteristic of progressions used by writers such as Donald Fagen and Walter Becker (of Steely Dan), Michael McDonald, and David Foster. Used with triads, they create a rich, contemporary pop sound used by artists ranging from country singers such as Tracy Lawrence and John Michael Montgomery to rockers such as Don Henley and Jon Bon Jovi.

The effect of these extensions and alterations is extremely subtle and, like arrangers' modulations, they are often added or deleted in the process of recording. In some cases, however, they create a unique sound that gives a song its characteristic flavor and as such

103

are an important tool for us to study. We're first going to look at how these extensions and alterations are created theoretically, and then we're going to explore how some of today's top writers have made use of them.

Extensions and Alterations Defined

Let's begin our exploration by taking a look at the C-major scale.

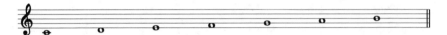

Notice that the notes in this scale occur in linear fashion; each note comes directly after the note that precedes it in the alphabet. If you were to play the notes in this scale up the keyboard of a piano (or the fretboard of a guitar), each scale tone would be played in order. In referring to the individual notes of the scale, we call the note on which the scale begins the *tonic* or *root*, the next note the *second* (the D in the C-major scale), the next note the *third*, etc.

Chords, with a few exceptions such as the dominant seventh sus 4 and the major and minor sixths, are always built in intervals of thirds (review Chapter 6, if necessary). Therefore, the notes in the C-major scale, as we would use them in forming chords built on C, would look like this.

In this example, the D, F, and A occur *above* the C–E–G–B that form the basic 1–3–5–7 of a chord built on C. Because the interval between C and D is now a major ninth rather than a major second (see Chapter 5 if you need to review this explanation), we call the D the *ninth* in any chord with C as its root. Similarly, an F would be called an *eleventh* and an A a *thirteenth*. It's important to remember that, like intervals, these extensions of the basic 1–3–5–7 chord are derived from the *major* scale of the root of the key. Thus, the ninth of a chord built on E would be F *sharp*, because F is sharped in the key of E, and the eleventh of a chord built on F would be B *flat*, because B is flatted in the key of F.

Alterations are extensions of basic triads or seventh chords that include notes that are *not* part of the major scale of the root of the chord. For example, in a chord built on C, a D♭ would be called a *flat ninth* or an F♯ a *sharp eleventh.* Similarly, an F natural would be a *flat ninth* against any chord with E as its root (because F♯ is the natural ninth), and a B natural would be a *sharp eleventh* as part of any chord with F as its root (because B♭ is the regular eleventh in that key).

Available Extensions and Alterations

Years ago I was working as the music director for the legendary Peruvian singer Yma Sumac, who has a vocal range of more than five octaves. At one point, we were having difficulty working on a particular song, and Yma suggested we abandon it because it was "out of her range." When I asked her how this was possible, given her range of more than five octaves, she smiled at me and said, "Yes, but not every note sounds good in every octave in every song." Similarly, although there are a wide number of extensions and alterations available to us as music writers, not every one will sound good with every chord in every tune. Certain extensions and alterations, as a rule, sound best with certain chords.

The following table illustrates the extensions and alterations that work well with the five chords most commonly found in contemporary popular music: the major and minor triads and the major, minor, and dominant sevenths. Extensions and alterations are rarely used with more "exotic" chords such as the augmented triad or minor major seventh because the sound of these chords themselves provides sufficient contrast with the more "ordinary" major and minor chords.

COMMONLY USED EXTENSIONS AND ALTERATIONS

Chord	*Extensions/Alterations*
Major triads and major sevenths	9, ♯11
Minor triads and minor sevenths	9, 11
Dominant sevenths	9, ♭9, ♯9, ♯11, 13

There is often confusion about the way some of these chords are notated, particularly in the case of triads. I have seen no fewer than *four* different ways to describe a major triad with an added ninth. The next table shows the way these chords are most frequently referred to in the industry. It's important, however, especially when analyzing songs from sheet music, to verify that the system of notation the arranger uses conforms to this standard.

Chord Symbol	Explanation
C9	C (dominant) seventh with a ninth
Cmaj9	C-major seventh with a ninth
Cm9	C-minor seventh with a ninth
C (add 9)	C-major triad with a ninth
Cm (add 9)	C-minor triad with a ninth
C2 or Csus2	C triad with a ninth and no third (C–D–G)
Cm11	C-minor seventh with an eleventh
C13, C7($\flat$9), C7($\sharp$11)	C dominant seventh with the designated extension and/or alteration

The term "C11" is often mistakenly used to denote a C7sus4. This is incorrect because an eleventh implies that the natural third is also present, which would be very discordant. In a C7sus4, the so-called "eleventh" *replaces* the third, and is therefore considered a suspended *fourth*.

Playing Extended and Altered Chords

Although an extensive discussion of the subject is beyond the scope of this book, it is necessary at this point to say a few words about how to play or *voice* these extensions and alterations. Because it is generally most comfortable for the guitar or the right hand of the piano to play four notes, there is no problem when adding single extensions or alterations to triads; one simply plays the three notes of the triad plus the extension or alteration. The case of seventh chords, where there are already four notes in the chord, is a different matter.

The most important color notes in a seventh chord are the third (which tells you whether it is major or minor) and the seventh. Extensions, then, are generally substituted for either the root or the fifth of the chord, depending on which is closer. Most commonly, the ninth will take the place of the root, and the eleventh or thirteenth will be played in place of the fifth. Thus, a C ninth chord (C dominant seventh with a ninth) could be voiced on the piano in one of these two ways.

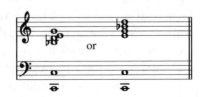

On a guitar, it might be voiced in one of these two ways (the numbers next to the notes indicate string numbers).

Those of you who are more experienced guitarists or keyboard players should have little problem voicing any of these chords with extensions or alterations. If you are less experienced on your instrument, you should seek the guidance of a competent piano or guitar teacher to help you learn to effectively perform these extended and altered chords, so that you can begin to use them in your writing.

Write out the following chords and play them on your instrument: Bm9, G(add9), A♭maj9, D7(#11), B♭13, Fm(add9), E7(#9), F#m11, E♭2, Cmaj7(#11), A7(♭9). Pay close attention to the sound of each one, and check your results against those in the appendix. Make sure you have a thorough understanding of the theory behind these extensions and alterations before going on to the rest of the chapter. It is permissible (and in most cases necessary if you're a guitarist) to select a different order of notes from that in the appendix, provided that the notes themselves are the same. The first example has been completed for you as a guideline.

Extensions and Alterations in Action

Extensions and alterations are used to add warmth and richness to individual chords within a progression. While this effect is often profound, its addition or deletion will not affect the basic relationship of the harmony to the melody and lyric. We're now going to look at some examples of how a wide variety of contemporary songwriters have made use of these extensions. Play them through both as written and substituting "regular" triads and sevenths, and pay close attention to the difference the extensions make. In every case you'll hear that, although the chords and melody work well together without them, the extensions have a significant impact on the overall sound.

Triads with Extensions

The addition of the ninth to a major triad, creating what is known as an "add 9" chord, is a device frequently found in contemporary music. Steve Dorff, composer of hits such as George Strait's "I Cross My Heart" and Kenny Rogers' "Through the Years," says that when he sits down to compose at the piano, his fingers almost instinctively fall on this chord. Listen to the introduction of Tracy Lawrence's 1993 number 1 country hit, "Can't Break It to My Heart" (co-written with Kirk Roth, Elbert West, and Earl Clark) and you can hear the guitars alternating between this add 9 chord and the plain major triad. We also find it throughout the work of contemporary rock and pop writers like Don Henley and Diane Warren in places where a richer sound is desired.

The minor triad is also frequently used with an add 9, creating an unusual and poignant effect. Listen to the introduction of the Billy Ocean ballad "Suddenly" (co-written with Keith Diamond) or Carly Simon's "That's the Way I Always Heard It Should Be" (co-written with Jacob Brackman) for a sense of the sound of this chord.

An interesting variation of the use of the ninth with triads is the so-called "2" chord (sometimes referred to as a "sus 2" chord), in which the ninth actually *replaces* the third. Because there is no third present, the chord is neither major nor minor and has a unique hollow-sounding quality. It can be found in the openings of Mr. Mister's "Broken Wings" and the Jon Lind/John Bettis collaboration "Crazy for You," which Madonna took to number 1 on the pop charts in 1985. Bruce Springsteen also used it to help create the haunting feeling of his 1994 Oscar-winning "Streets of Philadelphia."

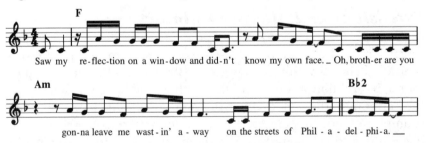

Play the song both with and without the "2" chord (substituting a plain B♭-major triad) and notice how the omission of the third and addition of the ninth help create the dark mood that underscores the poignant lyric about a man dying of AIDS.

Extensions of the Minor and Major Seventh Chords

The most common extension of the minor seventh chord is the addition of the ninth to form what we call the *minor ninth* chord. Like the addition of the ninth to the minor triad, it creates a distinctive sound that is best appreciated by listening. It is frequently used to reinforce the ninth in the melody, as in the example below from Al Green's "Let's Stay Together" (co-written with Willie Mitchell and Al Jackson), which was both a number 1 hit for Green in 1972 and a Top 40 hit when rerecorded by Tina Turner in 1984.

The *major ninth* chord (major seventh with a ninth) is also prevalent in today's pop and R&B, particularly in romantic ballads like Kool and the Gang's "Joanna" or Michael Bolton's "Missing You Now" (co-written with Diane Warren and Walter Afanasieff). Play the example below from the verse of "Missing You Now" both with and without the ninth added to the major seventh chord in the third measure to better appreciate the subtle difference in tonality of this chord.

Although the raised eleventh ($\sharp$11) on a major seventh chord is fairly common in jazz arrangements, its use in pop is quite limited. However, we often find the natural eleventh played with a minor seventh chord to form what is called a *minor eleventh*. This chord can be heard at the beginning of the chorus of "Missing You Now" as well as in the opening vamp and verse of Stephen Bishop's "On and On," where it creates prosody by giving the music an unusual, exotic flavor that corresponds to the Jamaican locale of the lyric.

Extensions and Alterations of the Dominant Seventh Chord

Throughout the history of popular music, the dominant seventh has been important because of its tendency to push a musical phrase toward completion as it resolves to the tonic (or to its target chord if it is a secondary dominant). Because of its unique harmonic structure, it supports the widest variety of extensions and alterations of any chord, as we noted in the table on page 105.

Like the major and minor triads and seventh chords, its most common extension is the ninth. Examples of the dominant ninth chord occur quite frequently; in fact, you may substitute a dominant ninth in virtually every situation where a dominant seventh chord is found and simplicity of sound is *not* desired. Writers whose music is more complex and harmonically sophisticated tend to include this sound in their songs more than those writing basic pop or country. Examples of songs that use the dominant ninth include the 1979 Grammy winner for both Song and Record of the Year, the Doobie Brothers' "What a Fool Believes" (co-written by Michael McDonald and Kenny Loggins), as well as much of the work of jazz-influenced rock groups such as Steely Dan and Toto. However, its use is not limited to that type of music. It can also be found in contemporary country and pop ballads where richer harmony is desired, such as Clint Black's "A Bad Goodbye," which he recorded in 1993 as a duet with Wynonna.

Thirteenth chords as well as dominant sevenths with altered extensions such as $\sharp 9$, $\flat 9$, $\sharp 11$, etc., have an even more dense and "jazzy" harmonic effect than dominant ninth chords. Listen to the sound of the thirteenth chords in the prechorus of Sheryl Crow's 1994 Record of the Year Grammy winner, "All I Wanna Do" (co-written with Wyn Cooper, Bill Bottrell, David Baerwald, and Kevin Gilbert).

Examples of altered dominant seventh chords (both the dominant seventh ♯9 and the dominant seventh ♯11) can be found in the bridge of Billy Joel's 1987 duet with jazz/blues master Ray Charles, "Baby Grand," in the section that begins with the lyric "But only songs like these played in minor keys . . ." Although "songs like these" are most commonly associated with the work of jazz composers such as Duke Ellington and Errol Garner, modern-day writers such as Billy Joel, David Foster, Walter Afanasieff, and Stevie Wonder have kept them consistently on the pop charts as well.

ASSIGNMENT

Write a song that uses at least four different extensions and alterations, including extensions of both triads and seventh chords. Then take one or more of the songs that you have written for previous assignments (or any song you have written) and try adding extensions and alterations to some of the chords. Begin to develop a sense of when they sound best to you—in what context and with which chords.

Wrap-Up

In this chapter we have explored how we can make the basic major and minor triads and major, minor, and dominant sevenths richer and more full sounding by using extensions and alterations. This technique, combined with the use of inversions and modulation that we discussed in the two previous chapters, gives us an almost unending variety of tone colors with which to vary the building blocks of pop harmony we looked at in Part III.

As you continue to analyze your favorite songs on the radio, notice how the writers use these techniques, and begin to incorporate them into your own writing. You will become increasingly aware of what a profound difference they can make. Because all composers have the same basic chords to work with, the use of these advanced variations contributes greatly to a writer's individual style. As you become more familiar with these devices and decide where you do and do not want to use them, your own unique sound will begin to emerge.

Part Five

The Melody

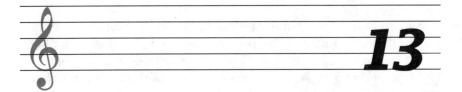

13

Choosing the Pitches

I magine the sound of a I major chord in the key of A♭. Now imagine it lasting for two beats, followed by a VI minor (F-minor) triad for two beats, a III minor (C-minor) triad for three beats, and a V7 of IV (A♭ dominant seventh) for one beat. While this may be difficult to do, the exercises you've completed in the previous twelve chapters should help you to hear the sound of this chord progression in your mind.

Now imagine the beginning of the melody of the Harold Arlen/Yip Harburg classic "(Somewhere) Over the Rainbow." Notice how much simpler it is for you to bring this melody to mind than the A♭–Fm–Cm–A♭7 chord progression that normally accompanies it. If it's that much easier for you, a practicing songwriter, imagine how much more quickly an untrained listener can bring to mind a melody than a chord progression. In fact, as we discussed in Chapter 1, many people refer to the entire musical component of a song as the "melody" because they are unaware of the harmony and its effect.

The *melody* of a song is actually *the part that the singer sings and the listener most directly identifies with.* As Preston Glass, writer of such hits

115

as Natalie Cole's "Miss You Like Crazy" and Aretha Franklin's "Who's Zoomin' Who" puts it, "The public, even though chords do affect them, doesn't care about an E minor or whatever. For them, it's 'What am I going to sing?'" This reflects one of the basic differences between writing melodies for hit songs and composing chord progressions. While chord progressions can be "crafted" and chord substitutions intellectually inserted without sounding contrived to the listener (such as when we added the secondary dominants to the Boz Scaggs melody in Chapter 9), a successful, memorable melody must sound spontaneous and natural.

In the next three chapters, we're going to learn a number of technical devices we can use to enhance the quality of our melody writing. Bear in mind, however, that there is no set formula for creating an interesting melodic line, and that these techniques are only methods to augment and fine-tune your own creativity and imagination in coming up with strong, singable melodies for your songs.

As we discussed at the beginning of Chapter 4, melodies occur in both space (pitch) and time (rhythm). Although most of them have a "natural flow" in which these dimensions are more organically combined, we are going to arbitrarily separate them into these components so we can examine them more effectively.

In this chapter, we'll look at the different aspects of choosing the pitches. The next chapter will be devoted to melodic rhythm, and the following chapter will cover motifs and motivic development, a particular combination of those pitches and rhythms.

Scales Used to Create Melodies

One of the principal differences between songwriting and classical composition (instrumental or operatic) is that pop songs by nature *must* be more singable. Indeed, the very selling point of a hit song—its musical hook (see Chapter 2)—demands that the average listener be able to sing along.

Although there have been some successful adaptations of classical melodies to pop music (such as The Toys' "A Lover's Concerto," whose melody was borrowed from Bach's "Minuet in G" by Linzer and Randell, and Eric Carmen's 1976 hit "All by Myself," which borrows from Rachmaninoff), the vast majority of pop, R&B, and country melodies have their basic roots in the tradition of English and American folk music.

Because of this, these melodies tend to be written almost entirely within the major scale of the key of the song (or the key of the moment, if the song modulates). The chief exceptions to this rule occur when the composer uses nondiatonic harmony, and the melody includes the nondiatonic tones contained within those chords. For instance, the Oscar-winning Bill Medley/Jennifer Warnes duet "I've Had the Time of My Life" (co-written by Franke Previte, Donald Markowitz, and John DeNicola, from the motion picture *Dirty Dancing*) is written in the key of E and begins with a flat VII D chord over an E pedal point. The melodic phrase accompanying that harmony (with the lyrics "I've been waiting for so long" and "I've finally found someone") consists of repeated D *naturals* and C sharps. The D natural in the melody, which is outside of the key of E, is used rather than the diatonic D sharp because it is part of the D/E harmony.

The Pentatonic Scale

Very often pop melodies are derived from a more simplified version of the major scale known as the *pentatonic scale*. This scale consists of a major scale without the fourth and seventh degrees (the *tritone* that we discussed in Chapter 8). Illustrated below is the pentatonic scale in the key of C.

Hum or sing this scale several times or play it on your keyboard or guitar and you will immediately begin to recognize its characteristic quality. An example of a melody derived entirely from the pentatonic scale can be found in Alan Jackson's 1993 Country Music Association Song of the Year "Chattahoochee."

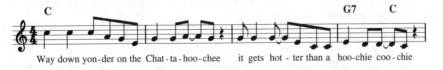

Way down yon-der on the Chat-ta-hoo-chee   it gets hot-ter than a hoo-chie coo-chie

Try singing the first two measures using this alternate melody which incorporates the seventh and fourth and you will be able to clearly hear the difference in sound between the pentatonic and major scales.

Way down yon - der on the Chat - ta - hoo - chee

Melodic Intervals

We're now going to examine the importance of *intervals* or *distances between notes* in composing melodies. (If you need to review the theory behind intervals, see Chapter 5.) As melody writers, we have a choice to use either *unison, stepwise motion* (movement by seconds), or a wider *intervallic leap* between any note and the following note. Passages that primarily use stepwise motion tend to flow more smoothly, whereas passages that feature larger intervallic leaps tend to sound more dramatic. To hear the effect of that difference, compare the Beach Boys' 1988 number 1 hit "Kokomo" (by Mike Love, Terry Melcher, John Phillips, and Scott McKenzie) with the example below from Sting's "If I Ever Lose My Faith in You."

If I ev - er lose ___ my faith ___ in you ___

If you listen to the Beach Boys' melody, you will find that it moves entirely in a stepwise fashion (except for two unisons), which underscores the easygoing lyric about "getting away from it all" to a tropical paradise where everything is laid back. Sting's melody, on the other hand, is far more dynamic with two leaps of a fourth and a jump from G to high B on the word "lose." This helps emphasize the more dramatic message of his lyric.

Merely using an intervallic leap, however, does not necessarily guarantee power or emphasis on the notes involved. Four additional factors help determine the effect of an interval:

1. *The size of the interval:* Generally the larger an interval is, the stronger it will be. Thirds sometimes have an almost stepwise quality (particularly within the pentatonic scale), while fifths, sixths, and sevenths are much more dramatic.
2. *Rhythmic placement of the notes:* When the second note of an interval falls directly on or on an anticipation of one of the strong beats in

the measure (like the word "lose" in Sting's song), the effect of the interval is more pronounced. In melodic analysis, the first and third beats in 4/4 and the first beat in 3/4 are considered strong beats.

3. *The duration of the notes involved*: When the notes involved in a leap are of longer duration (such as quarter or half notes), the effect will be felt more strongly than when the notes go by more quickly (such as eighth or sixteenth notes).

4. *The direction of the leap*: in general, ascending intervals (such as the leap to the word "lose" in "If I Ever Lose My Faith in You") have a more dramatic effect than descending intervals.

An example where all four of these characteristics come into play occurs in the chorus of Melissa Manchester's 1979 hit, "Don't Cry Out Loud" (music by Peter Allen and lyrics by Carole Bayer Sager). The key interval in the hook title of the song between the words "don't" and "cry" is an *ascending* large interval (a perfect fifth). In addition, both notes last a full beat and the second one falls on an anticipation of a strong beat.

Now compare it with the opening interval of Lionel Richie's "Lady," which was Kenny Rogers's longest-running number 1 hit, an A dropping down a perfect fifth to a D. If you sing the two melodies back to back you'll notice how much more understated the melody of "Lady" is than that of "Don't Cry Out Loud." That's because, although the intervals are exactly the same (a perfect fifth), the leap in "Lady" is descending, the first note lasts only for a half beat, and the second note falls on a weak beat.

To recap, intervals are extremely important in determining the quality of a melody. In general, the more intervals used and the wider the intervallic leaps, the more dramatic a melody will be. It's also important to take into consideration the direction and rhythmic placement of the interval and the duration of the notes involved. Finally, as with any other aspect of music writing, remain aware at all times of prosody. Dramatic lyric thoughts (such as "Don't cry out loud" or "If I ever lose my faith in you") are generally better underscored by use of stronger intervals, whereas more low-key lyrics (such as those in "Kokomo") are best given to more stepwise melodies or weaker intervallic leaps. Remember, too, that when using strong ascending intervals, the word on the highest note of the interval (such as "lose" in the Sting song or "cry" in the Melissa Manchester tune) should be a word that you want emphasized.

Write three eight-bar melodies. In the first, imagine that you are accompanying a lyric describing a humorous or mundane situation and use mostly stepwise motion. In the second, imagine that you are accompanying a highly dramatic lyric and make frequent use of strongly emphasized intervals. For the third, try describing a more "in-between" situation using a few intervals of smaller distance that are less accented. See if you can create melodies that, through their use of intervals and stepwise motion alone, create these emotional effects without accompanying lyrics or harmony.

Melodic Range

The term "range" refers to *the span between the highest and lowest notes in a melody.* Tunes where this distance is more than a tenth (an octave plus a third) are said to have a wide range, while tunes whose melody spans less than an octave are said to have a relatively narrow range.

Before discussing some of the more technical considerations of choosing an appropriate melodic range, let's first consider the most obvious one: *be certain that the melodic range of the song you're writing is compatible with the vocal range of the singer who's going to sing it.* For those of you who are writer/artists and intend to perform and record your own material, this is a relatively simple process; if *you* can successfully sing the melody, it is within your range. For those of you who are "outside writers" (that is, you write primarily for other recording artists), this is an extremely important consideration. Some artists, such as Mariah Carey, Whitney Houston, and Michael Bolton, are comfortable with extremely wide ranges and in fact may reject a song as not exciting or challenging enough if the range is too narrow. On the other hand, many singers will balk at performing a song with a wide range. Furthermore, it is important to remember that, as Yma Sumac told me in the anecdote mentioned in Chapter 12, not every note sounds good in every part of a singer's range.

Generally, if your songs have a range between an octave and an octave and a third, and do not dwell extensively on both the highest *and* lowest notes of that range, you are in fairly safe territory. If you have any doubts and are not a singer yourself, find a friend who is and have him or her perform the melody to ensure its singability before you invest your time and money in a demo.

The Importance of Contrast

As we discussed briefly in Chapters 2 and 3 when we looked at the Bon Jovi hit "Livin' on A Prayer," contrast in melodic range is one of the key devices for holding a listener's attention. In a verse/chorus song, the range of the notes in the verse will generally be lower than that of the chorus. Most often the high note in the chorus is only a third or at most a fourth above the peak note of the verse, yet this difference creates a profoundly dramatic effect. Examples of songs that fall into this category include such diverse tunes as Melissa Etheridge's "Come to My Window," "Hard Rock Bottom of Your Heart" (recorded by Randy Travis), and Jimmy Buffett's classic "Margaritaville."

It's not necessary, however, for the chorus to contain the melodic peak of a song. In some songs that employ a prechorus (see Chapter 2), that section of the song is the point at which the melodic range is highest, thereby providing contrast with both the verse that precedes it and the chorus that follows. Examples of this include Don Henley's "The Last Worthless Evening" (co-written with John Corey and Stan Lynch) and the Michael Clarke/John Bettis collaboration "Slow Hand," which was a pop hit for the Pointer Sisters, as well as a country hit for Conway Twitty.

Finally, on songs with a bridge, whether in A-A-B-A form (such as Stevie Wonder's "Part Time Lover") or verse-chorus with bridge (such as U2's "One"), the high point of the melodic range is often reserved for the bridge section, whose main purpose is to provide contrast with what has gone before.

Tessitura

In addition to the overall range of a song, it is important for us to be aware of the musical term "tessitura," which refers to the *general placement or position of pitches within the melodic range.* Melodies in which most of the notes occur in the higher sections of the range are said to have a high tessitura, while melodies with the majority of notes in the lower part of the range are said to have a low tessitura. Contrast in tessitura is as important, if not more important, than contrast in overall melodic range—that is to say the notes that are emphasized in a particular section of a song have as much significance as the actual highest and lowest notes.

An excellent example of contrast in tessitura occurs in the Carole King classic "Will You Love Me Tomorrow?" (co-written with Gerry Goffin), which was originally recorded by The Shirelles in 1961 and has since become a pop standard. The song is written in

A-A-B-A form, and the ranges of the verse and bridge sections are nearly identical—the verse going from F# to E and the bridge from G to E. The verse, however, begins near the bottom part of that range.

Except for the sixth and seventh measures (on the words "so sweetly"), the entire melody stays in this same general area (between F# and C).

The bridge, on the other hand, begins at the very top of the range.

It continues in the same register and, in fact, more than two-thirds of the pitches in the bridge are the two highest notes used in that section, E and D. Thus, while there is very little contrast in melodic *range* between the verse and bridge of this song, the contrast in *tessitura* makes it more interesting and has helped it become an enduring standard in the pop repertoire.

> Choose two or three of the songs you selected for the structural analysis assignment on page 12 in Chapter 2 and either buy the sheet music or take the melody down off the record. Notice both the range and the tessitura of the melody in each section (verse, chorus, prechorus, and/or bridge), and be aware of the contrast created by the difference in these elements.

Melody-Harmony Relationships

As I explained in Chapter 1, no discussion of melody is complete without examining its interaction with the harmony that supports it. You can give the same melody, with the same intervals and range, a completely different effect by altering the accompanying harmony. For example, sing the following melody or play it on your keyboard or guitar.

You may or may not recognize this melody, but in either case sing or play it again with the following harmonic accompaniment.

Notice the simple, almost "sing-song" effect, as though it were perhaps from a children's nursery rhyme. Now listen to the difference when the same melody is played with its real harmonic accompaniment.

Just a small town girl on a Sat-ur-day night _ look-ing for the fight of her life __

The melody is now clearly recognizable as the beginning of the verse of Michael Sembello's number 1 hit "Maniac" (co-written with Dennis Matkosky), from the movie *Flashdance*. With this harmonization, it has an unusual, intense, almost sinister quality. That's because the $F\sharp$, which falls on the downbeat of the first three measures, creates an eleventh and a ninth against the C/E and Em6 chords. These extensions have a much more exotic quality than the third, which was the function of the $F\sharp$ against the D-major triad in my first harmonization.

The following table can be used as a rough rule of thumb for judging how consonant or exotic a particular note will sound on the basis of its relationship to the chord of the moment.

Most Consonant ⟶ *Most Exotic*

3rds	Roots & 5ths	7ths & 6ths	Extensions

Songs in which the melody is composed primarily of roots, fifths, and especially thirds of the harmonic accompaniment tend to sound sweeter and more simple. The verse of Jack Tempchin's "Peaceful Easy Feeling," recorded in the '70s by the Eagles and in the '90s by Little Texas, is a good example.

I like the way __ your spar - klin' __ ear - rings __

lay   a - gainst _ your   skin _____ so __ brown, __

Notice that, with the exception of the G# in measure six, all the notes that fall on strong beats (the first and third beats) or are anticipations of those beats are chord tones of the accompanying E, A, and B-major triads. As a result, the melody has an easy-going quality that is in keeping with its title and lyrical message.

Let's compare the feeling that this song gives us with the opening eight measures of the Dino Fekaris/Freddie Perren collaboration "Reunited," which was recorded by Peaches & Herb and topped the charts for four weeks in 1979.

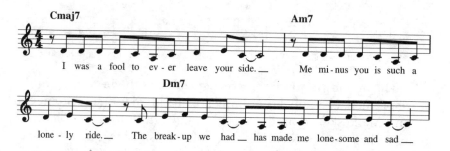

Listen to the quality of the melody in this song. While it contains no large intervallic leaps or unusual rhythms, it is still quite dramatic. This is due almost completely to the relationship of the melody to the accompanying harmony. The first measure starts on and repeats a ninth (a D against a Cmaj7), and the third measure uses an eleventh in the same way (the D against the Am7). In addition, the fifth and sixth measures each begin on a ninth and resolve to a seventh on the anticipated third beat. This gives the melody a haunting and unusual quality that would not be present were these notes roots, thirds, or fifths.

Try playing this melody, substituting chord tones for extensions (for example, E instead of D in the first measure) and listen to the difference. You'll become immediately aware of the extreme importance of melody/harmony interplay when choosing the pitches for your melodies.

Write two original melodies to the chord progression below using the melodic rhythms indicated but choosing your own pitches. Have the first melody consist primarily of roots, thirds, or fifths of the accompanying harmony, particularly on strong accented beats. In the second melody, use more sevenths and/or extensions on these beats and observe the difference in the sound.

ASSIGNMENT

Write an original melody with words and harmonic accompaniment. Make certain there is contrast in range and/or tessitura between the sections. Use intervals and melody/harmony relationships to create prosody between the melody and the lyric.

Wrap-Up

In this chapter we've looked at a number of factors that influence our choice of pitches in the melodies we write. We have discussed scale considerations, intervals between notes, range and tessitura, and melody/harmony relationships. While all this technical information is extremely valuable, the most important thing to keep in mind is that we are creating melodies to be *sung* and enjoyed, and a skillfully executed technical exercise in melody writing doesn't necessarily make for a memorable melody. In fact, I recommend that my students *not* try to consciously employ these techniques *as* they're writing a melody, but rather let it emerge on its own terms, and then use these concepts to strengthen it if it's weak.

Angela Kaset, writer of Lorrie Morgan's best-known hit "Something in Red" and a recording artist in her own right, put it like this: "The most important quality of a melody is the emotional feeling it conveys. As you learn the 'rules' of melody writing, they become like a sieve in your brain that you run everything through. But the problem even with the sieve is that you can get into self-editing before the inspiration has had a chance to fully develop. You don't start dressing up your baby before it's even born. You have it, it's born, then you examine it and put clothes on it so it looks the way you want it to."

14

Melodic Rhythm and Phrasing

Now that we've studied the various factors involved in choosing the pitches of a successful melody, we're going to look at what is known as the *melodic rhythm*, or placement of those pitches in time.

Throughout my years of teaching songwriting, I've found weakness in effective use of melodic rhythm to be one of the most common deficiencies of beginning songwriters. Frequently a student will play a song for me that has a solid verse and a well-written chorus, yet somehow there is no "magic." Often one of the reasons for this is that the student has failed to use *contrast* in melodic rhythm between the sections of his or her song. Virtually every hit in the last three decades, from pop to country to hard rock to R&B, whether rhythmically simple or complex, features some sort of contrast in this area.

We're now going to examine in depth the various aspects of melodic rhythm that we can use to create contrast. Our study will primarily concern itself with two areas: the qualities of the individual notes in a melody and the way those notes combine to form groups known as phrases. While a thorough knowledge of these principles will not guarantee you a hit song, it will certainly help you to avoid perhaps the most common pitfall in melody writing.

Rhythmic Accents

Think of the hook of the Righteous Brothers's "You've Lost That Lovin' Feeling" (co-written by Barry Mann and Cynthia Weil). Now imagine the beginning of the chorus of the Eagles' "Hotel California" (co-written by group members Don Henley, Glenn Frey, and Don Felder). Now bring to mind the hooks of Madonna's 1986 hit "Papa Don't Preach" (written by Brian Elliot with additional lyrics by Madonna) and Babyface's 1994 chart-topper "When Can I See You (Again)." Although these hits span four decades, they all have one thing in common: a distinctive and "catchy" set of rhythmic accents to the notes of the hook melody that make it virtually impossible to forget. Even if your hooks don't have memorable melodic rhythms like these, a working knowledge of the various possibilities in the realm of rhythmic accents will help you create effective contrast between sections.

The first type of rhythmic accent we're going to examine is the so-called "straight" rhythmic pattern, where all the accented and emphasized words fall *on the beats of the measure*. With this type of melodic rhythm, notes between the beats are used primarily to connect those that fall on the beat. An example occurs in the chorus of Diane Warren's "If You Asked Me To," which was a Top 10 hit for Celine Dion in 1992.

The opposite of so-called "straight" rhythm is what we refer to as *syncopated* rhythm, where most of the important notes fall on offbeats or anticipations of strong beats. This type of rhythmic accent pattern occurs quite frequently in contemporary music, as in the chorus of Toad the Wet Sprocket's "All I Want," which was a Top-Twenty hit in the same year.

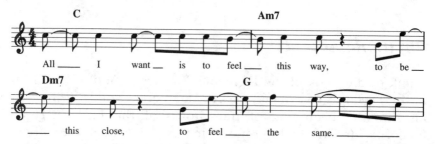

Notice that the notes accompanying the emphasized lyrics ("all," "want," "feel," "way," etc.) fall on anticipations of strong beats rather than right on the beat. Listen to the difference in feeling between the melody of this song and that of "If You Asked Me To" that is created by these "pushes."

It is important to remember that neither type of melodic rhythm is inherently superior to the other, only that interest is created by alternating them throughout the course of a tune. An excellent example of this variety occurs in the Burt Bacharach/Hal David classic "Walk On By," as recorded by Dionne Warwick. The verse begins with a more regular rhythm (like that of "If You Asked Me To").

The hook, however, is quite syncopated, with two of the three notes falling on the offbeats.

The effective use of contrast is one of the factors that have enabled writers such as Bacharach to continue to write hit after hit through the years.

Note Durations

Another simple and effective way of creating contrast in melodic rhythm is by altering the *number* of notes per beat. Melodies that make extensive use of sixteenth notes, or even long passages of repeated eighth notes, have a completely different feeling from those built on quarter, half, and whole notes. For example, listen to the chorus of John Michael Montgomery's 1994 country hit, "Be My Baby Tonight," written by Ed Hill and Rich Fagan.

Notice that the first two measures contain sixteen notes—the maximum number of eighth notes that could possibly be squeezed into that space. Now compare it with the beginning of the chorus of another country hit of the '90s, Joe Diffie's "John Deere Green" (written by Dennis Linde), which contains only three notes (plus a slur) in the same number of bars.

As with the choice of rhythmic accents, there is no "magic" number of notes per bar that will guarantee a great melody. What *is* important is that the different sections of a song include notes with a variety of durations to retain the attention of the listener. A song that does this most effectively is the Michael McDonald/Kenny Loggins collaboration "What A Fool Believes," which won a Grammy for Song of the Year in 1979 as recorded by McDonald's band, the Doobie Brothers. Although the song is written in a basic eighth-note groove (see Chapter 19) and does not make use of any sixteenth notes, the melodic rhythm of the verse is still quite busy, with eighth notes outnumbering quarter notes by more than three to one, and only one pause in the entire first six and a half measures. The pre-chorus (the section that begins "She . . . had a place in his life"), on the other hand, features several whole notes and extended rests, which provide relief from the more active verse melody. This is a prime example of the effective use of contrast in note duration.

Create a melody for the verse and chorus of an original song and deliberately *avoid* using contrast in melodic rhythm. In other words, have your verse match the rhythmic accents of your chorus, whether regular or syncopated. Similarly, whether your chorus uses many or few notes per beat, use notes of the same general duration in the verse. Play the final result and notice how weak and uninteresting it sounds. Now alter the verse melody to create rhythmic contrast. If the melodic rhythm in your chorus is more regular, have the new verse be syncopated; if your chorus melody is busier, have the verse melody be more open, etc. Notice how fresh the entrance of the second section now sounds. Bear this in mind and begin to apply it to all your writing.

Phrasing

The notes in a melody can be grouped rhythmically into what we call *melodic phrases*, which are defined as *groups of notes punctuated by space on either side.* Generally, a phrase will be what a singer sings in one breath. It also usually (but not necessarily) comprises a complete lyric thought. To better understand musical phrasing, let's look at Gary Baker and Frank Myers' "I Swear," another John Michael Montgomery number 1 country hit that also topped the pop charts for 11 weeks in a recording by the vocal group All-4-One. Here is how the verse begins.

These opening measures consist of two distinct musical phrases. The first one accompanies the lyric "I see the questions in your eyes," and the second one the lyric "I know what's weighing on your mind."

Just as contrast in individual melody notes is important to successful songwriting, contrast in the use of melodic phrases is a key to making a song sound more exciting. There are two primary areas in which this contrast can be created: the *starting point* and the *length* of the phrase.

The Starting Point

One important aspect of musical phrasing is choosing where each phrase begins. There are three distinct places where a writer can start a phrase. The first of these is directly on the downbeat (first beat) of the opening measure of a section of a song. An example of this can be found in the chorus of Tom Petty's 1995 hit "You Don't Know How it Feels."

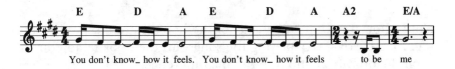

Notice how the first note of each of the first two phrases (the G accompanying the lyric "you") falls directly on the downbeat of the measure.

The second alternative is to have a phrase begin *before* the start of a bar. We refer to notes that come before the downbeat as *pick-up notes.* An example of a song whose phrasing makes use of these pick-ups is the Tom Snow/Cynthia Weil collaboration "He's So Shy," which was a Top 10 hit for the Pointer Sisters in 1980. Here are the first several measures of the verse.

Both the downbeat of the first measure (the word "saw") and the anticipated downbeat of the second measure (the word "speak") are preceded by three pick-up notes.

A third possibility for the rhythmic placement of a melodic phrase is to begin *after* the downbeat. This is often extremely effective in drawing attention to the melody, as the wait makes us eagerly anticipate what is to follow. Many songs with memorable melodic hooks, such as "You've Lost That Lovin' Feeling" and "Hotel

California," make use of this device. Foreigner used this delayed phrasing technique to reach the top of the charts with their 1985 hit "I Want to Know What Love Is," written by the group's guitarist, Mick Jones. These are the first four measures of the chorus of that song.

I want to know what love_ is____   I want you to   show __ me

Notice how the dramatic quality of the hook is underscored by the wait for its arrival. Try playing the song with the hook falling directly on the downbeat and listen to the difference.

There is, however, no hard-and-fast rule that a phrase must begin after the downbeat to be dynamic. Many powerful and dramatic hits have been written with hooks that begin either before or directly on the beat. The important thing is to be aware of *all* the options for beginning phrases and to use them appropriately.

Length of Phrase

The second factor we need to consider when dealing with melodic phrases is the *length* of the phrase. Very often a song that is quite inventive in terms of harmony, lyric, and choice of melodic pitch can tend to sound simplistic or rigid if all the phrases last exactly the same number of measures. Conversely, variation in phrase length can help a song sound fresh and dynamic. Let's look further at the 1994 ASCAP Song of the Year "I Swear," whose opening we examined earlier in this chapter.

With the exception of the brief two-note phrase accompanying the lyric "I'll stand," each of the phrases in the verse is between one and a half and two bars in length. The writers then begin the chorus like this.

I swear_   by the moon _ and the stars _ in the sky ___   I'll be there __

Listen to how the first chorus phrase (the hook title) provides a marked contrast to the longer verse phrases that precede it. The writers then employ a phrase similar in length to those of the verse, followed by another very short phrase ("I'll be there"). Then the entire three phrase pattern is repeated, followed by two one-measure phrases, another two-bar phrase, and a final repetition of the two-note hook title. This intricate variety of phrase length is part of the reason why "I Swear" became one of the most successful songs in the history of popular music.

In using phrases effectively, the name of the game is variety. It isn't necessary to make use of contrast in *both* length of phrase *and* starting point, but it is generally recommended to vary either one or the other. Thus, although almost all the phrases in "I Swear" start off the beat, the difference in phrase length that we discussed gives the song more than enough contrast. And though the phrases in both the prechorus and chorus of "You Don't Know How It Feels" are one measure long, the prechorus phrases start on pick-ups ("*so let's* get to the point") while the chorus phrases begin on downbeats. If you'll follow this simple rule of thumb and make sure that your songs have contrast in one or the other of these areas, you will save yourself from one of the most common pitfalls of unimaginative songwriting.

> Choose one of the songs you selected for the structural analysis assignment in Chapter 2 and either take down the melody or purchase the sheet music. Then mark off each phrase in pencil and write down both the length of the phrase and whether it begins on, before, or after the downbeat. Determine in which of these areas contrast is used, and notice the effect it has on you as a listener.

ASSIGNMENT

Write an original melody (with lyrics if you feel so inclined) for an entire verse/chorus song. Limit yourself to the five notes of the C pentatonic scale and do *not* use any harmony for the time being. By limiting the choice of pitches and taking away the possibilities of *harmonic* contrast, you'll be forced to use the different areas of melodic rhythm and phrasing that we have discussed in this chapter to create variety between the verse and chorus sections. Then, once you have completed this basic melody, harmonize it and feel free to alter the notes using other scale tones and/or notes outside the C-major scale as dictated by the harmony to complete your final version.

Wrap-Up

In this chapter we have explored the techniques you can use to rhythmically place notes in the melody of a song. We've looked at possibilities in the areas of both rhythmic accent (regular vs. syncopated) and note duration (many or few notes per bar). We've also looked at the possibilities for creating contrast in the way melodic notes are grouped into phrases. We've examined the use of differing lengths of phrases as well as several alternatives as to where they can begin (on the downbeat, after the downbeat, or using pick-ups). This study is valuable, but it won't serve us unless we constantly keep in mind that an understanding of melodic rhythms and phrasing is *only* useful when it helps to create a memorable and singable melody. Remember, these devices are not a substitute for creativity, but rather a way of bringing greater freshness and originality to the development of already interesting musical ideas.

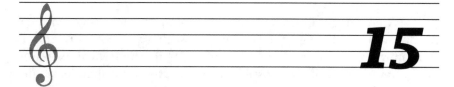

Motifs and Motivic Development

Perhaps the best-known and most easily recognized theme in classical music occurs at the beginning of Beethoven's Fifth Symphony. Consisting of four notes in the key of C minor— three eighth notes on a G natural followed by a half note on E♭—this unique grouping of notes is what we refer to as a *motif*. A motif can be defined as *a distinctive melodic figure upon which a section of a musical composition is built.*

In pop songwriting, a motif gives the listener a repeated phrase to remember as he or she hears a song for the first time. The opening measures of the choruses of "You've Lost That Lovin' Feeling," "Hotel California," "Papa Don't Preach," and "When Can I See You (Again)," cited in Chapter 14, are excellent examples. A motif may be as brief as one note (such as the shouted hook of the Michael Gore/Dean Pitchford hit title song from the movie *Fame*), or as long as ten notes or more (as in "Hotel California"). Individually, each motif has all the properties of pitch and melodic rhythm discussed in Chapters 13 and 14, including intervallic content, melody/harmony relationship, note durations, rhythmic accents, and starting point within the measure.

135

When you get that first melodic inspiration for a song, whether you're walking through the park or just sitting alone in your room, it usually comes in the form of a motif. While theoretical exercises for generating motifs are possible and perhaps even valuable, it's my personal belief that the most interesting and memorable melodies result when the basic motif has come purely from creative inspiration. Once this motif has been established, however, you can then make use of your technical knowledge to fully develop it into a well-crafted verse, chorus, or bridge section of a song. This is the process we're going to be explaining in this chapter.

Repetition and Alternation

The first and perhaps most obvious way to develop a motif is to repeat it one or more times. Sometimes the lyric is repeated along with the melodic motif, as in the chorus of Trisha Yearwood's "She's in Love With the Boy" (written by John Ims). In other songs, each repetition of the melodic motif is sung with a different lyric. We can find an example of this in Carly Simon's 1974 hit, "Haven't Got Time for the Pain," (co-written with Jacob Brackman), where the hook motif is first heard with the title, then with the lyric "Haven't got *room* for the pain," and finally a third time with the lyric "Haven't the *need* for the pain."

Sometimes writers will follow the original motif with a second motif before returning to it. This occurs in Ritchie Cordell's "I Think We're Alone Now," which was a Top 10 hit for Tommy James & The Shondells in 1967 and a number 1 hit for Tiffany twenty years later. Here are the first four measures of the chorus.

Notice that, although the second phrase ("There doesn't seem to be anyone around") has some pitches in common with the first, it is truly a separate motif. Cordell then returns to the first motif, which accompanies the lyric "I think we're alone now," and repeats the lyric verbatim. He completes the chorus by returning to the *second* motif, but *changing* the lyric to, "The beating of our hearts is the only sound."

Generally the motif accompanying the hook title reappears at some point or other in the chorus of a verse/chorus song. It can be repeated immediately, as in "She's in Love With the Boy," or after the entrance of a second motif, as in "I Think We're Alone Now." In some cases, such as Dan Fogelberg's tribute to his father, "Leader of the Band," *several* phrases are inserted before the original motif is repeated, and occasionally the hook motif occurs only once in the entire section. This is particularly true in A-A-B-A songs such as Crystal Gayle's "Don't It Make My Brown Eyes Blue?" (words and music by Richard Leigh), where the title's only appearance is at the end of each verse.

Addition and Subtraction

It is quite common in contemporary hit songs for a motif to reappear in a slightly altered version. This device enables the writer to maintain freshness and originality while still holding the listener's interest.

One of the most common ways to accomplish this is through a device known as *addition,* or adding pitches to the original motif. We can find a successful example in Eddie Money's first hit, "Baby Hold On" (co-written with Jimmy Lyon). The chorus consists of one motif repeated four times, but varied by means of addition. Here is the section in which we hear the motif the first two times.

The second appearance of the motif is exactly the same as the first, with the exception of the *addition* of the F accompanying the lyric "what" on the second half of the second beat in the third measure. While this may seem like an extremely subtle variation, try playing or singing this example without that syllable (so that you're singing "Baby hold on to me . . . ever will be will be") and notice the effect of the added eighth note.

The opposite way to vary a basic motif is through *subtraction,* wherein one or more notes are *removed.* A song that makes use of this device is Glenn Frey's "You Belong to the City" (co-written with Jack Tempchin). Following the title, the second line of the chorus ("You belong to the night") repeats the hook motif exactly, except in this case the last eighth note (the second syllable of the word "city") has been *deleted.* Try singing this example through, adding an additional note to the repetition of the motif (you may want to also sing an additional lyric such as "You belong to the night-*time*"), and the contrast created by subtracting this single note will become evident.

Changes in Pitch

Another way to modify a motif is to maintain the melodic rhythm but alter the pitches. Andrew Lloyd Webber uses this technique in "Memory" from his hit musical *Cats* (lyrics by Trevor Nunn).

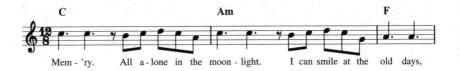

The original motif (the two dotted quarters on the lyric "Mem'ry") is first varied by the addition of five eighth notes ("All alone in the") as pick-ups. This altered motif is then repeated with the pitch of the last three notes changed from A, C, and C to G, A, and A. Try singing it using the same pitches for the words "the old days" as you do for "the moonlight" and listen to the difference.

In this song, only three notes in the motif are altered. It's also common, however, to alter the pitches of *all* the notes in a motif by playing them a step or two higher in the scale while maintaining the harmonic rhythm. This effect is used in the opening measures of Janis Ian's best-known song, "At Seventeen." The melody for the second phrase ("That love was meant for beauty queens") is exactly the same as the melody for the first phrase ("I learned the truth at seventeen") except that it occurs a whole step higher.

Melodic Contour

Although there is a change in pitch between the motifs in "Memory" and "At Seventeen," the *melodic contour* is maintained; that is, ascending motion and descending motion occur in the same places. Often, however, writers will insert a pitch change that alters the melodic contour, as I did in the hook of my country song "Lovin' You Is Killin' Me" (co-written with Siri Lee), which was featured in the 1995 film *Roosters* starring Edward James Olmos.

As you can see, in the first appearance of the motif the melody notes accompanying the lyric "lovin'" are played on the same pitch. When the motif is restated, however, I altered it both with the *addition* of the E on the lyric "is" and with a pitch change that features a descending leap of a fifth on the word "killin'." Play or sing the melody using the pitches E, E, and F# with the lyric "killin' me," and notice the effect created by the variation in melodic contour I used.

Change in Melodic Rhythm

Having listened to the sound of a motif when its melodic rhythm remains intact but its pitches change, we must now consider the opposite possibility, maintaining the pitches but *altering the melodic rhythm.* The late Boudleaux Bryant and his wife Felice used this technique at the beginning of the chorus of the Everly Brothers' first hit, "Bye Bye Love." After beginning the chorus with the three-note motif accompanying the title, the Bryants then expand it into the five-note motif accompanying the lyric "bye bye happiness." Then they repeat this augmented motif (accompanying the lyric "hello loneliness") but the entrance of the first note is *delayed* until the second beat of the measure. Try playing or singing this example twice, first as the Everly Brothers sang it and then using two half-notes in the fifth measure so the lyric "hello" falls right on the downbeat, and you'll hear the effect of this variation.

It's also possible to subtly alter *both* selected pitches *and* the melodic rhythm of a motif. The Nigerian/British vocalist Sade took home the Grammy as 1985's Best New Artist largely on the strength of her first hit, "Smooth Operator," which features such a variation. These are four measures of the chorus of that song.

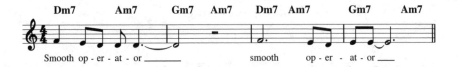

Notice that the motif accompanying the words "smooth operator" is repeated with a subtle variation in both rhythm *and* pitch. The first time, the word "operator" begins on the second beat and the motif ends on the anticipated fourth beat. In the second version, the word "operator" begins on the fourth beat of the first measure and does not end until partway into the second measure. In addition, the D on the last two syllables of that word has been replaced by an E. These variations (in particular the rhythmic variation) combine well with the Latin jazz-flavored groove of the song to help create its distinctive sound. It's important to remember in your own writing, however, that too many changes in both pitch and rhythm may result in the creation of an entirely different motif rather than the desired alteration of the original.

Harmonic Alterations

One final possibility for the alteration of a motif remains to be discussed, although it is not technically an alteration of the *melodic* motif. If you change the *harmony* the second time a motif appears, it will sound as though it has been altered even if the melody is repeated exactly. One of the best-known examples of this occurs in the first four measures of Sting's "Every Breath You Take," which won the Grammy for Song of the Year in 1983.

In this example, the melodic motif repeats exactly, but the second time the G on which it ends is harmonized with an E-minor chord rather than a G major. Although the melody itself is the same, the variation in the harmony creates effective contrast. Play the example through, first with a G-major chord on the last note of the second motif and then with the E-minor, and observe the difference.

Copy the following melodic motif onto a piece of staff paper six times, each time followed by two blank measures. Play or hum it through several times until you're thoroughly familiar with its sound. Then create six possibilities for the first four measures of a chorus, all of which use this motif for the first two measures. On the first variation, have the third and fourth measures of the chorus consist of this motif with *addition*. For the second variation, alter this motif through *subtraction*. For the third and fourth sample choruses, use the same melodic rhythm but vary the pitch, maintaining the melodic contour for the third variation and altering it for the fourth. On the fifth version, keep the pitches exactly the same, but use variation in the melodic rhythm, either by adding or deleting syncopation. Finally, for your sixth chorus, try a subtle variation in both pitch *and* rhythm that still maintains the flavor of the original motif. Some examples have been completed for you in the appendix, but they're not the only possibilities. Remember that the most important thing in completing this assignment is to make sure all your examples are *musical*, in addition to being technically correct.

Motivic Development

So far we have looked at very specific isolated instances of how a particular motif can be altered. In reality, however, motivic development is a vast and complex process. Most sections of songs have at least two motifs, each of which can be varied in any of the above ways. If we give each motif a letter name for the sake of analysis (calling the first to appear "A," the second "B," etc.), a wide range of combinations are possible, such as ABAB (as in "I Think We're Alone Now"), AAABB (as in "She's in Love with the Boy") or even ABABABCA (as in Hootie and the Blowfish's 1995 hit "Let Her Cry"). While it is common for a third and even a fourth motif to be added at some point, sometimes an entire chorus or even an entire song, such as Alan Menken and Howard Ashman's Oscar-winning "Beauty and the

Beast," can be built upon a single one. Furthermore, each time a motif returns it may come back in its original form or with any of the variations we have been discussing.

We're now going to analyze the motivic development in the chorus of a song that topped the charts in 1989—Richard Marx's "Right Here Waiting."

The chorus begins with a five-note motif accompanying the lyric "Wherever you go," after which the motif is repeated with different pitches and a change in melodic contour. Marx then brings in a "B" motif with the lyric, "I will be right here waiting for you." Next, the "A" motif is repeated twice, once as it originally appeared and once with the same alteration used in the second measure. Finally the "B" motif is reintroduced with changes both in pitch and in harmonic accompaniment (the A-minor chord at the end replacing the C). The resulting AABAAB pattern with its variations is an outstanding example of how motivic development can be used to create a well-crafted and musically interesting chorus that helps the song become a number 1 hit for the writer.

ASSIGNMENT

Choose two or three of your favorite melodies and either buy the sheet music or transcribe them from the recordings. Feel free either to continue using songs originally selected for the structural analysis assignment in Chapter 2 or to select new ones. Analyze each section (verse, chorus, etc.) in terms of motifs and motivic development. Notice how many motifs are used and in what order (AAB, ABAB, etc.). Notice also whether each motif comes back in its original form or in one of the altered forms we have discussed in this chapter. Begin to develop a sense of which of these variations most suit *your* musical taste, and start to consciously apply them to your own writing.

Wrap-Up

In this chapter we have examined in detail the different ways motifs are used in contemporary music. We have looked at some of the ways a single motif can be varied—including addition, subtraction, and melody and/or pitch changes—as well as how one or more can be developed to create a complete section of a song.

While it's virtually impossible to underestimate the importance of this aspect of melody writing, it's equally important to remember that motivic development is not a purely theoretical exercise, but rather a device whose failure or success can only be gauged by the freshness and singability of the melody that results. Alan O'Day, hit writer of such songs as Helen Reddy's "Angie Baby" and his own "Undercover Angel," puts it this way: "The craft and the rules are my stage, but when I'm writing I'm doing an ad-lib performance which might include bouncing off the ceiling or ripping the curtains apart. Sometimes cutting loose and taking a creative risk will produce a more powerful result than the most logically thought out melodic plan." It's extremely valuable to do exercises such as the one on page 141, but it's also important to keep them in this perspective.

Part Six

Writing in Minor Keys

16

Minor Scales and Melodies

Michael Jackson's "Billie Jean," Phil Collins' "Another Day in Paradise," Garth Brooks' "The Thunder Rolls," Carole King's "It's Too Late," and Mariah Carey's "I Don't Wanna Cry" have two things in common: they were all number 1 hits and they were all written at least partially in a minor key.

So far, we have primarily dealt with songs written in major keys. Indeed, all of the examples chosen for our analysis of pop harmony in Parts III and IV were major-key songs. This is entirely appropriate, because the vast majority of both current hits and modern classics that have become pop standards fall into this category. Nevertheless, the importance of minor-key writing cannot be underestimated. It pervades all idioms, from R&B to hard rock to country to mainstream pop, and has yielded many of the most well-known and frequently recorded songs of the last thirty years. This includes not only those mentioned at the beginning of this chapter, but also many others referred to in Parts I, II, and V of this book including Bon Jovi's "Livin' on A Prayer," U2's "One," Michael Sembello's "Maniac," and Sade's "Smooth Operator."

147

We're now going to explore the various aspects of writing in minor key. This chapter will be devoted to a study of the different minor scales from which melodies of minor-key songs are drawn. Chapter 17 will deal with the various chord progressions derived from those scales that are used to harmonize those melodies. In Chapter 18, we'll look at how many of today's top songwriters have borrowed certain melody notes and chord progressions from minor keys to augment the choices available when writing in a major key.

Minor Scales

If you ask ten musicians to play a C-major scale, they will undoubtedly all play the same notes, C–D–E–F–G–A–B–C. Yet if you ask those same ten musicians to play a C *minor* scale, you may hear several different results. Indeed, it is most probable that several of them will respond, "Which one?" That's because many scales that begin on C are classified as minor.

Before we delve into exactly what these scales are, it is necessary for us to define two important musical terms: *relative* and *parallel.* Musically, the word "relative" is defined as *having the same key signature.* Thus, any minor scale that has no sharps or flats is considered *relative* to C major. "Parallel" is defined as *having the same tonic note.* Therefore, any minor scale that begins on C (i.e., any of the various C-minor scales) would be considered *parallel* to C major. Make sure you understand these two definitions thoroughly before going on with the rest of the chapter, as they will help to clarify what might otherwise be a somewhat confusing topic. Also, be aware that, as in Chapter 6, whenever we use the terms "lowered" or "raised" in reference to a note, it is assumed to mean by a half-step.

Generally, we can define a *minor scale* as *any scale that has a lowered third note compared with its parallel major.* Thus, any scale beginning on C that has a E *flat* would be considered a C-minor scale. Similarly, any scale beginning on D and having an F *natural* would be considered a D-minor scale, because its parallel major, D major, has an F *sharp.*

While there are at least seven types of minor scales available (not counting so-called "synthetic minor" scales for which possibilities are almost limitless), only three of them are frequently heard in contemporary music. We're now going to explore each of these scales and look at some examples of how they're used in hit songs.

The Aeolian Scale

Perhaps *the* most common minor scale is the *Aeolian* scale, sometimes called the *natural minor* or *pure minor*. The Aeolian scale is *a minor scale that has the same key signature as the major scale built on the note three half-steps above.* Thus, for example, a C-Aeolian scale would have the same key signature as $E\flat$ major (three flats: $B\flat$, $E\flat$, and $A\flat$) because $E\flat$ is three half-steps above C. A C-Aeolian scale looks like this.

There are two other ways to derive the notes in an Aeolian scale. Because $E\flat$ is the *relative major* of C minor (it has the same key signature), you could look at the Aeolian scale as being built on the sixth note of its *relative* major. Or you could say that the Aeolian scale has the same notes as its *parallel* major, except for lowering its third, sixth, and seventh notes. Thus, a C-Aeolian scale would be the same as a C-major scale (its parallel major), except that it would have an $E\flat$, an $A\flat$, and a $B\flat$. Feel free to use whichever of these three systems for deriving the scale that seems most natural and simplest for you.

An example of an Aeolian melody occurs in the 1984 dance hit "Let the Music Play," written by Ed Chisolm and Chris Barbosa and recorded by Shannon. These are the first measures of the verse and chorus of that song.

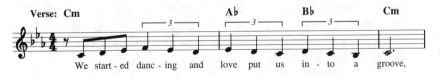

Notice the key signature of three flats in these examples. This is exactly the same as the key signature for E♭ major, yet as you listen you'll notice that the natural tendency of this melody, particularly in the verse, is to come to rest on C rather than E♭. This factor, combined with the C-minor chords on the downbeat of each section, clearly places this excerpt in C minor rather than E♭ major. Dance tunes, such as "Let the Music Play," have consistently been a source of much minor-key music of the last decade, from Donna Summer and disco to recordings by contemporary artists such as Janet Jackson and Madonna.

Write out the Aeolian (natural minor) scales built on the following notes: A, B♭, D, F, E, C♯, G, and E♭. Compare your results with those in the appendix, and make sure you have successfully completed them before continuing with this chapter.

The Dorian Scale

The next scale we're going to examine is the *Dorian* scale, which can be described as *an Aeolian scale with a raised sixth note.* The notes in the G-Aeolian scale (which is relative to B♭ major because B♭ is three half-steps above G) will be G–A–B♭–C–D–E♭–F–G. The G-Dorian scale, therefore, has a *raised sixth* (E natural) compared with its *parallel* Aeolian scale.

Notice also that this G-Dorian scale is *relative* to both D Aeolian and F major; that is, it has the same key signature as both of those scales. It is also the same as its parallel major (D major), with the exception of the *lowered third* and *lowered seventh* notes. Play or sing it through several times until you can hear the difference in the sound of this scale and its parallel Aeolian.

A great number of hit songs have been written using primarily the Dorian scale, such as the Norman Whitfield/Barrett Strong collaboration "I Heard It through the Grapevine," which topped the charts in the '60s for Marvin Gaye, was rerecorded in the early '70s by Creedence Clearwater Revival, and was featured in the '80s on *The Big Chill* soundtrack. More recently, the rap group Salt-N-Pepa and the R&B group En Vogue scored a Top Ten hit and a Grammy nomination with "Whatta Man" (by Dave Crawford, producer Herby Azor, and vocalist Cheryl James) which featured this repeated three-part Dorian melody.

What-ta man, what-ta man, what-ta man, what-ta might-y good man.

Try singing or playing this example through, both as it was actually written and then substituting E flats for the two E naturals in the lower part and for the one in the middle part on the final repetition of the word "man." The difference between the sound of the Dorian and Aeolian scales will become very apparent.

> Write out the Dorian scales built on A, B♭, D, F, E, C♯, G, and E♭. Use any one of the possibilities we discussed for deriving the scales: seeing the Dorian as its parallel Aeolian with a raised sixth, as its parallel major with a lowered third and seventh, or as a scale that begins on the second note of its relative major (G Dorian = F major). Compare your answers with those in the appendix and then play several parallel Dorian and Aeolian scales, one after the other, to cement the difference in sound into your mind.

The Blues Scale

The last of the three most common minor scales used in building today's melodies is known as the *blues scale.* This scale, like the pentatonic scale we discussed in Chapter 13, consists of only five notes. In this case, they are the first, *lowered* third, fourth, fifth, and *lowered* seventh notes in its parallel major scale. It's called the blues scale because the earliest improvised blues melodies were built on it. As a result, many of today's top instrumentalists, particularly guitarists, use it as the basis of their instrumental solos in all idioms of music, ranging from heavy metal to R&B to country. This is the blues scale in the key of A.

As you play or sing this scale, its sound should be quite familiar to you. Notice also that it actually has the same notes as the C pentatonic scale (see Chapter 13). Thus, a blues scale may also be derived by starting on the fifth note of its *relative* pentatonic scale, as well as by simply taking the second and sixth notes out of its *parallel* Aeolian or Dorian scale. There are numerous instances of its use in successful pop tunes. One of the best known occurs in Carole King's "It's Too Late" (co-written with Toni Stern) which was a hit both for Carole in the '70's and for Gloria Estefan in the '90's. Here is how the verse begins.

Listen to this melody on one of the recordings or play or sing it through several times, and pay attention to the sound of the blues scale. Notice also that the key signature for this song is the key signature of E *Aeolian,* just as the key signature for "Whatta Man" was that of G Aeolian. Because the Aeolian or natural minor is the most common of the minor scales, its key signature is generally used for all pieces in minor key, regardless of whether they are written in Aeolian, Dorian, blues scale, or one of the other variations or combinations we'll be discussing later on in this chapter. Thus, any song in E minor, whether written in Aeolian, Dorian, blues, or a combination of the three, would have the key signature of G major (one sharp), because G is the relative major of E Aeolian.

> Write out the blues scale built on B♭, D, F, E, C♯, F♯, G, and E♭ and check your results against the appendix. Try improvising with the notes in this scale, either instrumentally or vocally, and you'll almost instinctively start to duplicate the melodies of some of your favorite songs.

The Harmonic minor and Melodic minor Scales

There are two other scales, the *harmonic minor* and *melodic minor,* that were extremely common in the music of Bach and Mozart, but are seldom found in contemporary pop. It's still worth our while to study them, however, as we may occasionally want to give certain melodies a more classical sound, and because some of the chords derived from them (which will be discussed in the next chapter) are frequently used in a variety of styles today. The *harmonic minor scale* is formed by *raising the seventh note in the Aeolian scale*. Here's the C harmonic minor scale.

As you play or sing this scale, you'll notice the unusual augmented second interval between the sixth and seventh notes. The next scale we're going to look at is the *melodic minor* scale, where the sixth as well as the seventh is raised to eliminate this awkward interval. This is the C melodic minor scale:

Notice that this scale is exactly the same as its parallel major (C major) except for the lowered third. It is therefore the most major sounding of the minor scales. As I stated earlier, melodies derived from these scales tend to sound more traditional and classical, because eighteenth and nineteenth century composers used them (along with the natural minor) as the basis for the vast majority of their works in minor key. Songs such as Neil Diamond's "Love on the Rocks" (co-written with composer Gilbert Becaud) and much of the work of French composer Michel LeGrand (including "The Way He Makes Me Feel" and "What Are You Doing the Rest of Your Life?") are examples of contemporary works that incorporate the sound of these scales.

The Phrygian Scale

The last scale we're going to look at, which is rarely used in either contemporary or classical music, is the Phrygian scale. The *Phrygian scale* is *an Aeolian scale with a lowered second note*. Here are the notes in the C Phrygian scale.

You might also think of this scale as being built on the third note of its *relative* major (in this case, A♭ major). As you sing this scale or play it on your instrument, notice its unique, somewhat Spanish sound. It was used by songwriter Ervin Drake to create the unusual melody in the first four measures of Frank Sinatra's "It Was A Very Good Year."

> Write out the harmonic minor, melodic minor, and Phrygian scales built on A, B♭, D, E, and F, and compare your results with those in the appendix. While it is not necessary that you memorize the notes in these scales in all keys, it is important to become familiar with their sound so you can make use of them in your songs.

Writing Minor Melodies

All of the techniques of melody writing discussed in Part V apply equally to writing melodies in minor keys. In fact, many of the songs cited in those chapters are actually written in a minor key. As we stated earlier, however, there is no one minor scale from which these melodies are taken. All the scales we have discussed so far—including Aeolian, Dorian, blues, harmonic minor, melodic minor, and Phrygian—may be used individually *or in any combination* to create minor-key melodies. In fact, that is perhaps the most interesting aspect of writing in a minor key: *You may move freely from one minor scale to another within a single song.* One of the many successful examples of this occurs in Whitney Houston's hit "So Emotional" (co-written by Billy Steinberg and Tom Kelly, whose other hits include Madonna's "Like A Virgin" and Cyndi Lauper's "True Colors"). Here are the prechorus and first two measures of the chorus.

As you can hear (and tell by the key signature), the song is in the key of E minor. Yet the song uses both the E *Dorian* and *Aeolian*

scales. The $C\sharp$ accompanying the word "like" in the third measure of the prechorus comes from the Dorian scale, whereas the C natural that begins the chorus is from the Aeolian. The possibility of switching at any time from one scale to another is both one of the most liberating and one of the most challenging aspects of writing melodies in a minor key.

ASSIGNMENT

Write an original melody (with lyrics, if you desire) for a verse-chorus song in minor key. Remain in one key, but use at least two different minor scales within that key (such as Aeolian and Dorian or Aeolian and blues) in different sections of the song. Feel free to experiment with some of the less-common minor scales (harmonic minor, melodic minor, and Phrygian), but make sure at least part of your song uses either the Aeolian, Dorian, or blues scale. Apply all the principles of melody writing we studied in Part V in terms of melodic rhythm and phrasing, choosing the pitches and motific development.

Wrap-Up

In this chapter we have looked at the various scales that contemporary songwriters have used to create melodies in minor key. Remember that, while far fewer songs have been written in minor than in major, the majority of today's most successful artists have had at least one minor-key hit, and it is important to increase the options available to you as a composer by becoming familiar with the possibilities of writing in this tonality.

17

Minor-Key Harmony

In Chapter 16, we studied the scales from which songwriters create melodies in minor keys. In this chapter, we're going to explore the chord progressions used to harmonize those melodies. We'll study the techniques used by a wide variety of contemporary artists, from Michael Jackson and the Doors to Garth Brooks and Mariah Carey. In addition, we'll look at both the similarities and differences between harmony in minor and major keys.

Diatonic Harmony in Minor Keys

Just as in the major keys, the most frequently used chords in minor key are the diatonic chords. It was relatively simple to identify the *diatonic chords* in major keys as we did in Chapter 7, because there was only one scale from which to derive them. In minor, however, the possibilities for diatonic chords are far more complex because of the greater number of minor scales. We're now going to examine the various diatonic

156

chords available in minor keys. We'll then look at how these chords can be combined, both with one another and by use of some of the harmonic techniques discussed in Part IV.

Diatonic Chords in Aeolian

Let's begin our study of minor diatonic harmony by looking at the chords derived from the most commonly used minor scale, the *Aeolian* or natural minor. As we learned in the last chapter, the Aeolian scale is a minor scale with the same key signature as the major scale built on the note three half-steps above. Therefore, the notes in an A Aeolian scale would be the same as the notes in a C-major scale, which are all natural. Let's build the seventh chords diatonic to A Aeolian by constructing four-note diatonic chords on each note of the scale, much as we did for the major scale in Chapter 7.

A Aeolian

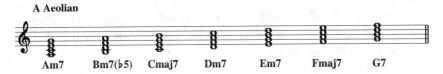

Am7   Bm7(♭5)   Cmaj7   Dm7   Em7   Fmaj7   G7

Remember that when we first introduced the concept of Roman numerals in Chapter 7, we said that they are derived from the *major* scale of the root of the key. This is true even when dealing with minor harmony: the Roman numerals are assigned on the basis of the *parallel major* of the minor scale we're discussing. Thus, the diatonic seventh chords in A natural minor would be Im7, IIm7♭5, ♭IIImaj7 (C is ♭III because C♯ is the third degree of the parallel major, A major), IVm7, Vm7, ♭VImaj7, and ♭VII7.

It is also true that whatever we say about seventh chords is also true for the triads they contain. Thus, the formula for the diatonic *triads* in Aeolian would be Im (Am), IIdim (B dim), ♭III (C), IVm (Dm), Vm (Em), ♭VI (F), and ♭VII (G).

We're now going to examine a song whose chorus is written using only diatonic chords from the Aeolian scale, Donna Summer's "She Works Hard for the Money" (co-written with her producer, Michael Omartian).

As you can see, all five chords used in the chorus of this song are diatonic to A natural minor, the Im (Am), ♭VII (G), ♭VI (F), IVm7 (Dm7), and Vm7 (Em7). More recently, Babyface and Daryl Simmons used these same chords to create the chorus of Toni Braxton's 1993 hit, "Another Sad Love Song."

> Write out the diatonic seventh chords and triads in both B Aeolian and F Aeolian on a sheet of staff paper. Begin by writing the Aeolian scale in each key and, using accidentals rather than key signatures, build up the diatonic seventh chords as we did for A Aeolian. Then analyze both the seventh chords and the triads they contain using Roman numerals, remembering to assign them based on the degrees of the *parallel major* scale, and check your results against those in the appendix before continuing.

Diatonic Chords in Dorian

Let's repeat the same procedure for the Dorian scale. Let's again work in the key of A, and start by writing the A Dorian scale in one octave. As we discussed in Chapter 16, the Dorian scale is the same as the Aeolian (natural minor) with the addition of a raised sixth, so the A Dorian scale will read A–B–C–D–E–F *sharp*–G. Now let's write out the diatonic seventh chords built on these notes and add both the names of the chords and their Roman numerals (remembering that Roman numerals are assigned on the basis of scale degrees of the *parallel major*).

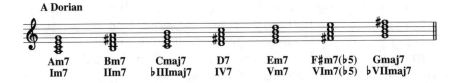

A Dorian

| Am7 | Bm7 | Cmaj7 | D7 | Em7 | F#m7(b5) | Gmaj7 |
| Im7 | IIm7 | bIIImaj7 | IV7 | Vm7 | VIm7(b5) | bVIImaj7 |

One of the first things you'll notice is that three of these chords, the Im7 (Am7), bIIImaj7 (Cmaj7), and Vm7 (Em7), are exactly the same as they were in natural minor. In addition, the *triad* built on the seventh degree (G) is the same as that of the parallel Aeolian. The only difference is that the major seventh is added to the chord in Dorian, whereas the lowered (dominant) seventh is added in natural minor.

Two of the chords that do not occur in the Aeolian scale, the IIm7 (and IIm triad) and the IV7 (and IV *major* triad), are chords considered characteristic of the Dorian sound. Rocking back and forth between the Im and any of the characteristic Dorian chords (IIm, IIm7, IV, or IV7) is a harmonic technique known as a *Dorian vamp*. Both "It's Too Late" and "Whatta Man," which we analyzed melodically in Chapter 17, are built on Dorian vamps, as are Traffic's "Low Spark of High Heeled Boys" and Simply Red's "Holding Back the Years." Another band that was especially fond of this sound was The Doors, who used it as the basis for such songs as "Riders on the Storm," "Soul Kitchen," "When the Music's Over," and the improvisation section in the middle of their most famous hit, "Light My Fire." In fact, it was a joke among schooled musicians at the time when The Doors were most popular that they chose their name because so many of their songs were built on vamps that were "Door-ian."

> Write out the diatonic seventh chords in B and F Dorian. As before, write out both the names of the sevenths and the triads they contain and their Roman numerals. Check your results against those in the appendix, and make sure that you fully understand the diatonic structures in both Aeolian and Dorian before continuing.

Diatonic Sevenths in Other Minor Scales

Although the harmonic minor, melodic minor, and Phrygian scales are not as important melodically, we derive several diatonic chords from them that figure quite prominently in minor-key harmony. Let's write out the diatonic structures in A harmonic minor, melodic minor, and Phrygian, and examine the resulting harmonies. Remember that the harmonic minor scale is the same as the Aeolian scale with a raised seventh note, the melodic minor is the same as the harmonic minor with a raised sixth, and the Phrygian is the same as the Aeolian with the addition of a lowered second.

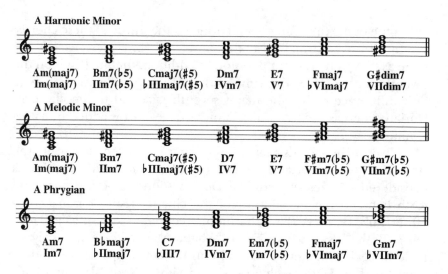

A Harmonic Minor

| Am(maj7) | Bm7(b5) | Cmaj7(#5) | Dm7 | E7 | Fmaj7 | G#dim7 |
| Im(maj7) | IIm7(b5) | bIIImaj7(#5) | IVm7 | V7 | bVImaj7 | VIIdim7 |

A Melodic Minor

| Am(maj7) | Bm7 | Cmaj7(#5) | D7 | E7 | F#m7(b5) | G#m7(b5) |
| Im(maj7) | IIm7 | bIIImaj7(#5) | IV7 | V7 | VIm7(b5) | VIIm7(b5) |

A Phrygian

| Am7 | Bbmaj7 | C7 | Dm7 | Em7(b5) | Fmaj7 | Gm7 |
| Im7 | bIImaj7 | bIII7 | IVm7 | Vm7(b5) | bVImaj7 | bVIIm7 |

The first thing you'll notice is that a large number of these chords are duplications of many of the diatonic structures we encountered in Aeolian and Dorian, such as the IVm7 and bVImaj7 in harmonic minor and Phrygian, and the IIm7 and IV(dominant)7 in melodic minor. Furthermore, several of these chords, such as the bIIImaj7#5 in harmonic and melodic minor and the Vm7b5 in Phrygian, are virtually never used in contemporary writing. However, a number of chords derived from these scales are quite important.

The Im(maj)7 chord found in harmonic and melodic minor is used as part of a Im–Im(maj)7–Im7 sequence at the beginning of many hit songs, ranging from Leon Russell's "This Masquerade" (as recorded by both Russell and George Benson) to Led Zeppelin's classic "Stairway to Heaven." In addition, both the bII and bVIIm chords from Phrygian mode are often used to harmonize melodies derived from the Phrygian scale, such as "It Was A Very Good Year," which we discussed in Chapter 16. But the most important chords by far taken from these lesser-used minor scales are the V7 and V major triad. (Again, everything we say about seventh chords is also true for the triads they contain.) These chords are as important in minor key as they are in major because of their strong pull to resolve back to the tonic I (in this case Im), as we will see in many of the examples cited throughout the rest of this chapter.

> Write out the diatonic chords built on the harmonic minor, melodic minor, and Phrygian scales in both B and F. Again, write the chord names for both triads and sevenths as well as the Roman numerals, and compare your results with those in the appendix to make certain you have a thorough understanding of the diatonic structures associated with these scales before continuing.

Mixing Diatonic Chords from Different Scales

In Chapter 16 we discovered that we can draw from a variety of scales when writing melodies in minor key. Similarly, when harmonizing minor melodies, we are completely free to mix chords that are diatonic to any of the minor scales. For example, one of Michael Jackson's biggest hits, "Billie Jean," which topped the charts for seven weeks in 1983, begins with an F♯ *Dorian* vamp.

The chordal movement here, which continues throughout the first four bars, is from F♯m (Im) to G♯m (IIm). In the fifth measure, however, Jackson moves to a Bm7 (IVm7) chord, which is diatonic to the *Aeolian* mode. He later begins his prechorus on a D (♭VI) chord and ends it on a C♯7 (V7), both of which come from the harmonic minor. Such mingling of harmonies diatonic to a variety of minor scales is not at all uncommon in minor-key writing. In fact, it is the norm.

> Here is an exercise that will synthesize the work we've done so far in this chapter by creating a master list of *all* the possibilities available for diatonic minor harmony. Draw a chart with seven columns, labeled with Roman numerals I through VII. In each column, write the names of *all* the available diatonic chords from the different minor scales that begin with that particular Roman numeral, including the lowered versions such as ♭III and ♭VI. For example, under I you would have Im, Im7, and Im(maj)7, etc. Feel free to omit any diminished triads as well as the chords that we stated earlier are

virtually never used in minor key, such as ♭IIImaj7♯5 and Vm7♭5. When you have completed this chart, compare it with the chart in the appendix and make certain they match exactly.

Harmonic Analysis in Minor

We're now going to discuss the harmonic functions of the diatonic minor chords on the chart we have created. As in major keys, the I, III (or in this case, ♭III), and VI chords (excluding ♭VI) are tonic, and the V and VII chords (excluding ♭VII) are dominant in function. The Vm chord, though not as dominant as the V or V7 chord because of the loss of the half-step motion from its third to the root of the Im tonic chord, still has a dominant quality. We can find an example in the prechorus of Patti LaBelle's 1985 hit, "New Attitude" (co-written by Bunny Hull, John Gilutin, and Sharon Robinson).

The song is in the key of B minor, and the prechorus starts on a Gmaj7 (♭VImaj7) before moving to the F♯m7 (Vm7), which leads into the chorus (the section that begins "I'm feeling good from my head to my shoes"). Try playing it with an F♯ *dominant* seventh instead of an F♯-minor seventh and notice the difference. You can hear that, although the F♯7 creates a more dramatic resolution, the F♯m7 is still dominant in function.

Subdominant Chords in Minor

Classifying subdominant chords in minor keys is different from classifying them in major because there are actually two types of subdominant chords built on the II, IV, and ♭VII. Those that are derived from the Aeolian scale and contain the *lowered* sixth note of the parallel major, such as IIm7♭5, IVm7, and ♭VII7 (as well as the ♭VI itself), are said to have a *minor subdominant* function. Those derived from the Dorian scale that have the *same* sixth note as the parallel major, such as IIm7, IV major, and ♭VIImaj7, are said to have a *major subdominant* function, because they are the same subdominant chords found in major keys. When analyzing songs, then, we use the symbol *SD* to denote chords that have a major subdominant function, and *SDM* for those that have a minor subdominant function.

Other Available Chords in Minor Keys

The diatonic chords we have looked at so far correspond to the diatonic chords in major keys that we discussed in Chapter 7. It is also possible to make use of chords similar to those in major keys discussed in Chapters 8 and 9. We have already looked at the ♭VII, which is actually diatonic to several of the minor scales. The V7sus4, or V triad sus 4, is also used in many minor-key songs, such as Dan Hill's "Can't We Try." In addition, it is possible to use *secondary dominants* (see Chapter 9) of *any* of the chords on the chart of minor-key possibilities we created, as Stevie Wonder does in the prechorus of his 1977 number 1 hit "I Wish."

The Big Four

Imagine that you're walking into a new restaurant where you've never eaten before. You open the menu and see six items. Most likely you would look each one over thoroughly and decide which of all the available choices you're most in the mood for before placing your order. Now imagine walking into another restaurant and seeing a ten-page menu with more than a dozen items on each page. Chances are, especially if you're hungry, you would look for an item familiar to you and order that, rather than reading the entire menu and examining all the possibilities.

An analogy can be made between these hypothetical situations and selecting a chord progression. Because, as we have shown, there are so many more choices available in minor keys than in major ones, contemporary writers tend to make repeated use of several of the most familiar of these chords rather than exploring all the possibilities. In particular, four chords are used more frequently than any of the others: the Im, the ♭VII, the ♭VI, and the V. Indeed, a large number of successful hit songs have been written using *only* combinations of these four triads and their related sevenths (Im7, V7, etc.).

One of the most common ways to utilize these chords is to play them in descending scalewise order (I to $\flat$VII to $\flat$VI to V). From classics such as Holland/Dozier/Holland's "Standing in the Shadows of Love" (recorded by the Four Tops) to rock tunes such as Mark Knopfler's "Sultans of Swing" (recorded by his band Dire Straits) this progression has been an important part of our musical heritage. These chords are often used in different combinations as well, as in the chorus of Garth Brooks's 1991 hit "The Thunder Rolls" (co-written by Pat Alger and illustrated below) where the progression goes from $\flat$VI (B$\flat$) to $\flat$VII (C) to Im (Dm), then from $\flat$VI to $\flat$VII to V7 (A7).

In addition, many songs use only three of these "big four" chords. Such diverse tunes as the Eurhythmics' "Sweet Dreams are Made of This" (co-written by singer Annie Lennox and guitarist Dave Stewart) and the verse of Francis Lai's "Theme from *Love Story*," are written using only the I, $\flat$VI, and V. Another extremely popular subgroup is the I, $\flat$VII, and $\flat$VI, omitting the dominant chord. Among the many songs built solely on these three chords are Gloria Estefan's "Rhythm Is Gonna Get You" (co-written with Enrique Garcia), recorded by her group Miami Sound Machine, and the chorus of Phil Collins's 1989 ode to the homeless "Another Day in Paradise."

Modulation in Minor Keys

Although it is quite common to confine the harmony in a song to combinations from within these "big four" chords, many writers compensate for the relative monotony of relying on such a limited number of chord changes by using modulation. This technique is far more common in minor keys than in major, for two basic reasons.

First, songs written in minor actually do sound "sadder," and by modulating to a major key for part of the song, this effect is somewhat alleviated. Second, because of the tendency to confine minor-key writing to the "big four" chords, modulation is an effective way to introduce different harmonies and create contrast. Dance tunes tend to be an exception to this, because their uptempo, exciting grooves provide a counterbalance to the "sad" harmony and effectively generate and maintain musical interest. Some of the songs discussed so far in this chapter that do modulate include "Another Sad Love Song," "This Masquerade," and "It's Too Late."

While it's possible to shift to virtually any key, two particular modulations are most frequently associated with minor-key music. The first of these is modulation to the relative major (considering the minor as the natural minor). This type of modulation tends to sound less abrupt, because most of the chords found in one key are also found in the other, and the tonal center is the only thing that really changes. Heart took advantage of this technique in its 1985 hit "What About Love" (co-written by Brian Allen, Sheron Alton, and Jim Vallance). The song begins in D minor with an introduction using the Im–$\flat$VII–$\flat$VI progression over a D pedal point, after which it goes into the verse (with the lyric "I've been lonely. I've been waiting for you"), with the chord progression Dm–B$\flat$–F–C.

As you play this chord progression through or listen to the recorded version, notice that, although all the chords are available in the relative major (F major), the D minor clearly *sounds* more like a I chord than the F. The song continues in that key, ending on the $\flat$VII (C) chord that is also the V chord in the relative major (F). It then breaks into the chorus ("What about love? Don't you want someone to care about you?"), where the chord progression is F/A–B$\flat$–C.

As you play or listen to the chorus, be aware of the difference in tonality. Although the same chords are used as in the verse (except for the D minor), you can hear that this section is clearly in F major. Thus, although only four different chords are used in the verse *and* chorus of this song, effective harmonic contrast is created because the verse is in a minor key while the chorus is in the relative major.

The second most common modulation in minor-key songs is to the *parallel major*. This technique was used by Brenda Russell in her 1988 hit "Piano in the Dark," (co-written with Jeff Hull and Scott Cutler), whose verse begins with this passage in the key of F minor.

The verse then continues with the ♭III (A♭), ♭VI (D♭) and ♭VII (E♭) chords and is followed by a second verse that ends on a V (C) chord. This chord functions as a pivot (see Chapter 11) because it is the dominant in both the keys of F minor and F *major*. The chorus that follows is written in major key.

The chorus remains in major until the final phrase where the hook title is sung, which ends on an Fm chord and sets us up for the return of the verse in minor.

While these modulations to the relative and parallel majors are by far the most common in minor-key songs, they are by no means the only key changes available. Roxette's "Listen to Your Heart," for example, begins in the key of B minor and features a bridge in the key of E major that leads to a return of the chorus in D# minor. As you begin to listen more closely to songs in minor and analyze them, you will become aware of more and more possibilities.

We are now going to study a number 1 hit that uses many of the techniques of minor-key harmony we have explored so far in this chapter: Mariah Carey's "I Don't Wanna Cry," co-written with Grammy-winning producer Narada Michael Walden. Copy the chart onto a piece of staff paper and analyze the song the same way you analyzed the examples in Chapters 7–11, writing the key followed by a colon at the beginning, the Roman numeral analysis above the chords, and the harmonic analysis above the Roman numerals. Refer back to Chapters 10 and 11 for specific discussion of how to treat inversions and modulations. Be sure to play the song through several times before beginning the analysis so that you're actually *hearing* it as you work. Compare your results with those in the appendix before continuing.

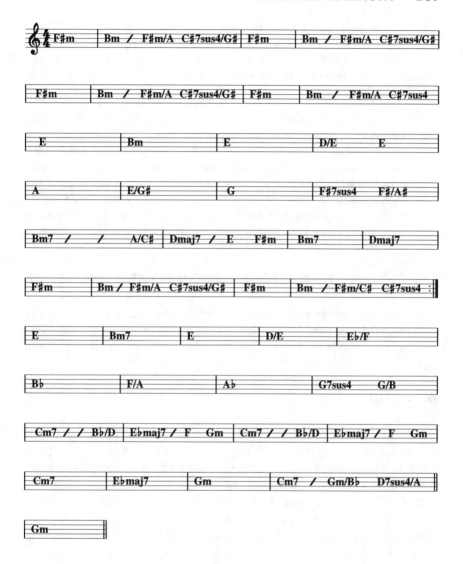

ANALYSIS

"I Don't Wanna Cry" begins with a repeated two-measure progression from the harmonic minor featuring the Im, IVm, and V7 (sus 4) chords with a descending bass line. The prechorus that follows both begins and ends on the ♭VII (E) chord, which is also the V chord in the relative major (A). The substitute sus (D/E) chord that precedes it strongly signals the modulation to the key of A in the chorus, which starts on a I–V–♭VII–V7 of II progression with the third in the bass of the V chord. After eight bars, the chorus lands on a Dmaj7 (IVmaj7) chord, which is also a $\flat$VImaj7 in the relative minor and heralds a return to that key. After the verse and chorus are repeated, we hear the prechorus with an altered melody ("All the magic's gone . . .") followed by a *direct arranger's modulation* to the final chorus in B$\flat$ and tag in G minor.

Notice how Walden uses chords derived from different minor scales (C#7 from harmonic minor, E from natural minor) in the verse and prechorus. Notice also the prosody created by having the discussion of the negative state of the relationship ("only emptiness inside us . . ." etc.) accompanied by harmony in a minor key, while the statement about the singer needing to leave and move on with her life ("I must find a way of letting go . . .") is written in major. This is an example of why quality songs in minor keys have become both hits and standards in all styles of music.

ASSIGNMENT

Write an original song in a minor key that modulates at least once to either the relative or parallel major. Use chords derived from at least two different minor scales (such as Aeolian and Dorian) to create harmonic contrast.

Wrap-Up

In this chapter we've examined the various ways in which the minor-key melodies we explored in Chapter 16 can be harmonized. We've looked at the diatonic structures derived from the Aeolian, Dorian, Phrygian, harmonic minor, and melodic minor scales, as well as the related V7sus4 and secondary dominant possibilities. We've discussed the so-called "big four" chords, which are the most frequently used in minor-key writing, as well as various possibilities for modulation. While this may at first seem like a vast amount of information, through continued study and analysis of songs written in minor keys as we did for "I Don't Wanna Cry," you'll begin to get a sense of how to integrate these techniques into your own personal style. Though you may never write a great number of songs in minor, having the ability will certainly make you a more versatile composer.

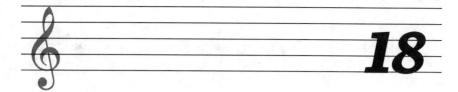

18

Borrowing from Minor in Major Key

Now that we've explored the harmonic and melodic choices available in minor, we're going to look at how a wide range of artists, from the Eagles and Diamond Rio to Jimi Hendrix and Nirvana, have found a way to incorporate them into their *major*-key songs. After making a thorough study of the material presented in this chapter, you should be able to integrate some of these possibilities into your own writing as well.

Melodies That Borrow from Minor Scales

One of the most common ways in which writers borrow from minor key in major is through the addition of notes derived from various minor scales to major-key melodies. Of these, perhaps the most common are the lowered third and lowered seventh found in the blues, Aeolian, and Dorian scales. Because they are diatonic to blues and minor scales, these notes tend to give *major* key melodies a more "bluesy" sound. An example of this occurs at the beginning of Robert Palmer's 1986 number 1 hit "Addicted to Love," illustrated below:

169

The lights are on | but you're not home | Your mind __ | is not your own

As you can see, the song is written in the key of A major, which has an F♯, C♯, and G♯, and the C♯ at the beginning of the first full measure is the diatonic third in that key. However, in the following two measures Palmer sings a C natural, the lowered third of the key. Try playing or singing the melody using C *sharps* rather than C naturals accompanying the words "you're" at the end of the second full measure and "not" at the end of the third, and you'll hear the bluesy quality that lowered thirds give to a melody. The G natural accompanying the word "mind" is borrowed from the blues scale as well, but also falls into the category of nondiatonic melody contained within nondiatonic chords (in this case the ♭VII G chord) that we discussed in Chapter 13. Other songs that make use of this technique of borrowing the lowered third from the parallel minor include John Hiatt's "Thing Called Love" (also recorded by Bonnie Raitt), the Pointer Sisters' "Neutron Dance" (co-written by Allee Willis and Danny Sembello), and the Eagles' 1994 comeback single, "Get Over It" (co-written by founding members Don Henley and Glenn Frey).

The Tonic Minor

As we discussed in Chapter 17, the ♭III chord occurs in both the Aeolian and Dorian scales and is tonic in function. It's often used to harmonize melodies in *major* key as well (particularly in rock), where its function is referred to as *tonic minor*. Whether or not the lowered third of the scale is also part of the melody, the tonic minor ♭III chord will tend to create a bluesy effect. It's found almost exclusively as a triad, since its diatonic seventh is a *major seventh*, which tends to counteract this quality. A classic example occurs in Jimi Hendrix's famous "Purple Haze," perhaps the best-known song from his debut album, *Are You Experienced?* These are the opening measures of the chorus of that song:

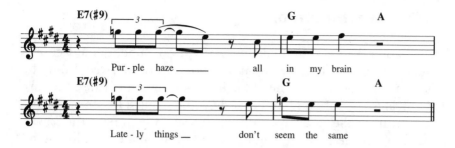

The song is written in the key of E major, and the G chord in the second and fourth measures is the tonic minor that we've been discussing. Notice that the melody in the fourth measure also includes the lowered third of the scale, while in the second measure it does not. Hendrix's I–♭III–IV progression is one of the most common contexts in which the ♭III is found. A variety of songs, ranging from Deep Purple's "Smoke on the Water" to Paul Simon's "Fifty Ways to Leave Your Lover," use the tonic minor in this context. It also appears in many of the hits Mick Jagger and Keith Richards wrote for the Rolling Stones in the late '60s and early '70s, including "Brown Sugar" and "Jumpin' Jack Flash," as well as in Nirvana's best known single, "Smells Like Teen Spirit."

> Write out the ♭III tonic minor chord in all keys (using C♯ and F♯ rather than D♭ and G♭) and check your results against those in the appendix. Try playing it in several of these keys in a I–♭III–IV progression, and notice the blues/rock flavor of the sound.

The use of the tonic minor is not by any means limited to rock and roll, however. Stevie Wonder's "Higher Ground" is but one of many R&B tunes that contain a ♭III chord. It's also frequently heard in adult contemporary songs, where an unusual and somewhat exotic minor-tinged flavor is desired, such as Barbra Streisand's "Evergreen" (co-written with Paul Williams), where it occurs in the bridge accompanying the lyric "unrehearsed." You can even find it in country hits with a blues/rock feeling, such as Diamond Rio's "This Romeo Ain't Got Julie Yet" (co-written by guitarist Jimmy Olander and Eric Silver).

Subdominant Minor

In Chapter 17 we identified the two types of subdominant chords found in minor key. We discussed both those derived from the Dorian scale, which are called major subdominant because they are identical to the subdominant chords in the parallel major, and those derived from the Aeolian or Phrygian scale, which have the *lowered sixth* note of the parallel major and are called minor subdominant, or *subdominant minor.*

Subdominant minor chords, which we can define as *chords that contain the lowered sixth of the key,* are the chords borrowed from minor that are most frequently found in major. Seven of these chords are commonly used: the IV minor family (consisting of the IVm triad, the IVm7, and the IVm6), the $\flat$VII7, the IIm7$\flat$5, the $\flat$IImaj7 (borrowed from Phrygian), and the $\flat$VI chord itself, which can be found in either its triadic form or as a major seventh. These are the subdominant minor chords in the key of G:

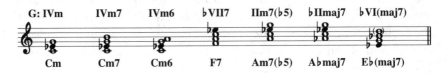

Notice that each of these chords contains the E$\flat$ or lowered sixth note of the key of G, and that all of them (including the IVm6, which we haven't discussed until now) are diatonic to either the G Aeolian or Phrygian scales.

> Before we begin our analysis of how these chords are used in contemporary music, write out the seven subdominant minor chords in the keys of A, B, C, D, E$\flat$, and F on a piece of staff paper. Check your results against those in the appendix, then play the I chord moving to each subdominant minor chord and back to the I in each key. This will help familiarize you with both the construction and sound of these chords and prepare you to work through the rest of this chapter.

The Unique Quality of the Subdominant Minor

To begin our exploration of the use of these subdominant minor chords, let's examine the first two measures of the Eagles' hit

"Desperado" (co-written by Don Henley and Glenn Frey), which was a hit video from their 1994 *Hell Freezes Over* album and concert tour and has also been recorded by many other artists, including Linda Ronstadt and Clint Black.

Des - per - a - do, why don't _ you come to your sens - es?

The song, which is in the key of G, begins on G major (the I chord) and then moves to the secondary dominant G7 (V7 of IV—see Chapter 9). The target chord, C (the IV chord) is immediately followed by the IVm6, a subdominant minor chord. Listen to the sound of each of these chords. The opening tonic G (I) chord is peaceful, while the dominant G7 (V7 of IV) creates motion that then resolves to the C or IV chord.

Now listen closely to the IVm6 or C-minor sixth chord. Because of its origin in minor key, it has a particular sound quality common to all subdominant minors, which you probably noticed when you played the chords you wrote out for the exercise on page 172. This effect is often described with words such as "poignant," "wistful," "nostalgic," "emotional," and "bittersweet" and is particularly important to us as songwriters in the context of prosody. Prosody, as you'll recall from our discussion in Chapter 3, refers to musically reinforcing the emotion that the lyrics convey. Often a writer can set this emotional tone by the use of a subdominant minor chord near the beginning of a song. The IVm6 at the end of the phrase "Why don't you come to your senses?" for example, reveals at least as much about the quality of life of this "desperado" as do the lyrics "You only want the ones that you can't get" and "You better let somebody love you before it's too late," which Henley and Frey use later in the song.

We find another interesting example of this effect in Marvin Hamlisch's "Nobody Does It Better" (with lyrics by Carole Bayer Sager), which Carly Simon sang as the theme of the James Bond movie, *The Spy Who Loved Me.* These are the opening bars of that song:

No - bod - y does _ it bet - ter ___ makes me feel sad ___ for the rest

This song is also in the key of G, and Hamlisch begins on the IV (C-major) subdominant chord and moves to the IVm (Cm) before resolving to the I or tonic chord. As you play or listen to this example, notice the poignant, bittersweet quality of the subdominant minor IVm chord. Now think for a moment about the lyric. The phrase "Nobody does it better" could be quite positive. After all, if nobody does it better than the singer's lover, this should be cause for celebration. Yet as we listen to the subdominant minor chord we realize that something is unfulfilling about their relationship. This subdominant minor harmony continues throughout the rest of the song, as Hamlisch uses six subdominant minor chords in the verse and chorus—almost one every other measure. Of course we know that the singer's love affair is unrequited because her lover is James Bond, who is off to his next conquest in his next picture, but notice that it is the subdominant minor *music alone*, rather than anything in the lyric, that conveys the sadness of this situation to us.

Other well-known hits that use these chords to create similar emotional effects include the David Gates/Bread classic "If" and Madonna's 1995 chart-topper "Take a Bow" (co-written with Babyface). However, although subdominant minor chords always have a poignant and emotional quality, it doesn't necessarily have to be a sad quality. Two places where these chords create a touching but not unhappy effect are the seventh measure of the chorus of "That's What Friends Are For," which we examined in Chapter 9, and the ending of Kenny Rogers' "She Believes in Me" (written by Steve Gibb), where the singer, referring to his lover who is keeping their bed warm while he works on his latest song, tenderly sings "While she waits . . . while she waits for me."

Subdominant Minor in Chord Progression

Subdominant minor chords are most frequently found in the harmonic context of subdominant to subdominant minor to tonic. The most common example of this is a progression going from IV (the most basic subdominant chord) to IVm or one of its variants IVm6 and IVm7 (the most common subdominant minor chords) to I (the basic tonic chord). The two excerpts from "Desperado" and "Nobody Does It Better," both contain this progression (the IVm6 in the second measure of "Desperado" is followed by a I chord on the downbeat of the third measure).

However, subdominant minor chords are not *always* used in this way. One instance of an alternate usage occurs in Toni Braxton's 1994 hit "You Mean the World to Me" (co-written by Babyface, L. A. Reid, and Daryl Simmons). Here is the beginning of the chorus:

The song is written in the key of F#, and the two subdominant minor chords Dmaj7 and Bm6/D (♭VImaj7 and IVm6) follow the *tonic* D#m (VIm) chord rather than a subdominant chord. This is done in conjunction with the E in the bass of the F# chord in the second full measure to create a descending 1–♭7–6–♭6 bass line. Babyface used this exact same bass line and chord progression (without the IVm6) to create the mood in the opening line of the Madonna hit "Take a Bow" mentioned earlier.

We are now going to analyze a classic song by the Bee Gees from the soundtrack of *Saturday Night Fever*, the haunting "How Deep Is Your Love." Be sure to listen to the original recording or play the chords through on your keyboard or guitar and hum the melody or sing the lyrics before beginning your analysis. Then harmonically analyze the song, writing the key with a colon at the beginning, the Roman numeral analysis above each chord, and the harmonic function above each Roman numeral (use "SDM" for subdominant minor chords). Compare your analysis with that in the appendix to make sure it is correct, and make some observations of your own about the effect of these subdominant minor chords in the light of what we've discussed so far before reading the next section.

ANALYSIS

The first subdominant minor chord to be introduced is the $D\flat7$ or $\flat VII7$ in the twelfth measure, coinciding with the first "sad" lyric, "Then you softly leave." In the subdominant–subdominant minor–tonic progression in the eleventh through thirteenth measures, the Bee Gees use substitution by function for the traditional IV–IVm–I, inserting a IIm7 (Fm7) in place of the IV, a $\flat VII7$ ($D\flat7$) instead of the IV minor, and a G minor 7 (IIIm7) in place of the I. If you play this song through using $A\flat$, $A\flat m$, and $E\flat$ to harmonize those measures, you will notice that, although the IV–IVm–I progression has a poignant feeling, it is not as harmonically rich as the substitution the Bee Gees used. Notice also the use of the subdominant minor $A\flat m6$ (IVm6) in the eighteenth and twenty-fourth measures and the $A\flat/B\flat$ (IV/V) substitute sus chord (see Chapter 10) in the fourth, eighth, and fourteenth measures.

ASSIGNMENT

Write a song with at least one subdominant minor chord and either the tonic minor $\flat III$ chord as part of the harmony or a lowered third or lowered seventh in the melody. Make certain, particularly when using the subdominant minor, that the music is appropriate to the emotion conveyed by the lyric.

Wrap-Up

In this chapter we have looked at the various ways contemporary songwriters have been able to incorporate melodies and harmonies derived from minor scales into their major-key writing. We have discussed the use of the lowered third and lowered seventh of the major scale in melodies, as well as the use of both the tonic minor and subdominant minor in chord progression. The wide variety of music we have cited is a clear indication of the importance of this aspect of writing in all styles of music. Like curry powder, it is an *exotic* spice that need not necessarily be used frequently, but should be in your "harmonic spice rack" so that you can freely make use of it when its effect is called for in a particular piece.

Part Seven

Putting It All Together

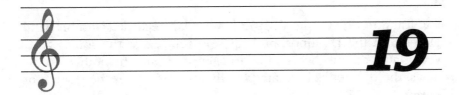

19

Rhythm and the Groove

Our work with minor keys in Part VI completes our inquiry into the melodies and chord progressions found in contemporary music. Virtually every song you hear on the radio—whether pop, R&B, country, adult contemporary, or hard rock and roll—is built completely on material that we have studied so far. Were you to examine sheet music for any of your favorite songs, you would find nothing more than the melodies and harmonies we've been discussing.

Yet there is a third element present that can neither be perceived from the written music alone nor copyrighted. This element, which we touched on briefly in Chapter 1, is in many cases as important as the melody and harmony in determining the impact that a song has on an audience. Listen, for example, to the instrumental openings of the first two cuts on side one of Michael Jackson's multiplatinum album *Bad*, the title cut and "The Way You Make Me Feel," both of which were number 1 singles. During their introductions, notice that, although neither the chord progressions nor the melodies have yet been established, you are immediately aware of a fundamental difference in the underlying feeling. That same difference is evident when

181

you listen to Eric Clapton's 1972 hit "Layla," recorded with his band Derek and the Dominos, and his solo remake of the song twenty years later on the best-selling *Unplugged* album. In both of these cases, the difference is created by what we refer to as the rhythm or *groove.*

What Is a Groove?

Before we establish a specific definition of "groove," let's look at what a groove is *not.* Groove has little to do with the time signature (see page 35 in Chapter 4), which basically tells you the *meter* or *number of beats per measure* in a song. Although a few hits have been written in 3/4 time, such as Natalie Cole's "I Live for Your Love" (by Alan Rich, Pam Reswick, and Steve Werfel) and Collin Raye's "Somebody Else's Moon" (by Tom Shapiro and Paul Nelson), over 95 percent of the songs on the radio today have four beats per measure, whether they are written in 4/4 or 12/8. We'll discuss the specific difference between these time signatures later in this chapter.

Groove also does not have to do with the *tempo,* or *number of beats per minute* in a song. While the number of beats per minute determines the actual speed of a verse or a chorus, it may not necessarily determine how fast the song *seems* to go by to the listener. For example, I was once called in to write and record some background music for a tape containing positive affirmations that people could listen to while jogging or doing aerobics. Because my goal was to create a rhythm that the producers felt was appropriate for accompanying physical activity, I played them two examples from an exercise video I had recently scored. One example had a BPM (beats per minute count) of 120 and the other a BPM of 132. Their response was quite surprising. They said they preferred "the faster one," even though they were actually referring to the one at 120, because it was written with an underlying groove that made it *seem* faster.

The term "groove," then, refers to *the underlying subdivision of the beat* in a particular song. Let's go back to the Michael Jackson and Eric Clapton examples we mentioned earlier. If you tap your foot on the beat of each of these songs, while simultaneously tapping out the subdivisions of the beat on a tabletop, you will find that your hands tap four times for every beat in "Bad" and the Derek and the Dominos version of "Layla" and three times for every beat in "The Way You Make Me Feel" and Clapton's acoustic version. That's because the basic subdivisions in "Bad" and the earlier "Layla" are sixteenth notes (of which there are four per beat) while the basic subdivisions in "The Way You Make Me Feel" and the unplugged "Layla" are triplets (of which there are three per beat). The following example illustrates this difference:

BASIC BEAT

SIXTEENTH-NOTE SUBDIVISION

TRIPLET SUBDIVISION

This distinction is very difficult to understand purely by reading the printed page, and I strongly recommend spending some time listening and tapping along to the above examples and/or analyzing songs on the radio before going on. Once you have a clear sense of the difference between the basic beat and its rhythmic subdivisions, the rest of the material in this chapter will be much easier to understand and integrate into your own writing.

The Drum Machine

The groove of a song can be established by any number of instruments, including the vocal. In fact, we'll spend some time in Chapter 20 discussing different ways to create a groove in a demo. In *this* chapter, however, we're going to confine our discussion to the instrument that most commonly establishes the groove—the drum kit.

From a three-piece rock group to a twenty-piece jazz big band, it is generally the drummer who is responsible for constantly defining the groove as well as the meter and tempo of a song. Technological advances made during the '80s, however, have enabled the songwriter to take on that function in his or her own living room through the use of drum machines. If you do not currently own a drum machine (or a computer/synthesizer/sampler set-up that includes drum sounds and a sequencer), I suggest you purchase at least an inexpensive one. Virtually every major songwriter today makes use of this new technology, even those who are band members and writing primarily for their own bands. It has become as essential a tool as the piano was during the '30s and '40s.

Because of the predominance of drum machines and their computer-based equivalents in today's writing, we're going to use them as the basis for our discussion of grooves in this chapter. Once you have programmed your drum machine to create the appropriate groove for the song you're writing, you can simply play along using whole-note chords on your keyboard or guitar, and your music will have the feel of the groove. Or, if you're a more competent and creative instrumentalist, you can play any number of chordal riffs and/or bass lines *against* that groove to make the rhythm even more interesting. In the event you have no access to a drum machine, you can still get a basic sense of the grooves we'll be discussing by tapping out the drum patterns with your hands and feet and then simulating their feeling as closely as possible on your guitar or keyboard alone.

One final word before we go on. Although a book on the subject would be a welcome addition to the literature available for songwriters today, it's beyond the scope of *this* book to give you specific detailed instruction in drum programming. I'm concerned only with your developing a sense of the underlying grooves that form the rhythmic framework for the melodic and harmonic material we've discussed in previous chapters. For that reason, we'll be limiting our discussion to grooves created by use of only the three most basic parts of the drum kit. Be aware, however, that most of today's grooves, especially in sophisticated dance music, are created by a wide variety of sounds in addition to, or in some cases even replacing, these three.

Drum Notation

The most important parts of the percussionist's kit are the bass or *kick drum*, the *snare drum*, and the *high hat*. The kick drum is generally played with the drummer's right foot, if he or she is right-handed, and usually (though not always) strikes on the downbeat of each measure, plus one or more additional times during the measure. The snare drum is almost invariably hit on the second and fourth beats, called *backbeats*, although occasionally it is omitted from the second beat or added in other places. The high hat (or cymbal in hard rock or jazz) is generally struck more frequently throughout the measure and used to spell out the basic subdivision. When writing for drums, the kick, snare, and high hat are notated as follows:

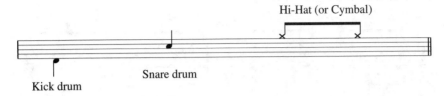

Bear in mind that on some of the examples we're going to cite, particularly the more contemporary ones, the actual "instruments" used may not be kick or snare drums or high hats, but rather sampled sounds that take the place of these instruments in the musical spectrum. For example, I had one of my songs released as a single on which the producer, Steve Cropper (himself a great writer whose credits include "Sittin' on the Dock of the Bay" and "In the Midnight Hour"), informed me that the "instrument" used for the bass drum was really the sequenced sound of a basketball striking a gym floor. Because of the technology available with today's sophisticated samplers, such practice is quite common.

Eighth-Note Grooves

The simplest groove commonly used in today's music is the *eighth-note groove*, in which each beat is subdivided into two equal parts. To create the most basic eighth-note groove possible on your drum machine, have the high hat play on every eighth note, the snare drum on two and four, and the kick drum on one and three (as well as under the snare on two and four if you wish). This groove, notated below, can be found in simple, straight-ahead rock or country tunes such as Don Henley's "The Last Worthless Evening" (co-written with John Corey and Stan Lynch) and Alan Jackson's 1993 recording of Robert Geddins and K. C. Douglas' classic "Mercury Blues."

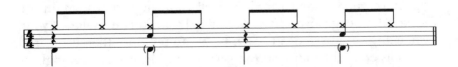

If you listen to REM's Grammy-winning 1991 hit "Losing My Religion," you'll hear the most common modification of this groove, which adds an additional bass kick on the second half of the second beat. It is notated like this:

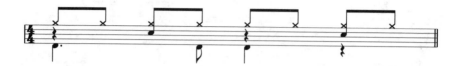

Among the many other songs that feature this variation are George Strait's "The Chill of an Early Fall" (by Green Daniel and Gretchen Peters) and Bruce Springsteen's rock anthem "Born in the U.S.A."

Eighth-note grooves work well in a wide variety of tempos, from as few as 70 to as many as 150 or more beats per minute. Using either of these two variations will give you a good basic rock or country feeling, while adding, deleting, and/or syncopating different percussion attacks will create more interesting rhythmic textures. For example, Sting used this eighth-note groove in his 1987 hit song "We'll Be Together Tonight":

As you listen to this example, notice the bass drum attacks in the second measure that are played an eighth note *before* the third and fourth beats. These anticipations create an interesting effect known as *rhythmic syncopation*, much like the melodic syncopation we discussed in Chapter 14. Engineer Hugh Padgham, who co-produces much of Sting's material, enhanced this effect in his 1994 remix of "We'll Be Together Tonight" for *The Best of Sting* album by also anticipating the downbeat of the second measure and having the high hat attack only on the second half of each beat. Such remixes are quite common today in all styles of music that use drum machines or computer-based sequencing to create their rhythmic foundations.

Once you've familiarized yourself with the three variations of the eighth-note groove we've examined, try making up some of your own, being certain to divide each beat into no more than two parts. As you listen to the radio, become aware of which songs have eighth-note grooves and try to take down some of the basic kick, snare, and high hat combinations so you can emulate and expand on the ones you like, using them as a rhythmic springboard to create your own melodies, harmonies, and lyrics.

ASSIGNMENT

Program the three eighth-note grooves diagramed in this section into your drum machine. Experiment with playing first one chord and then a series of chords against them at various tempos, ranging from 80 all the way up to 150 beats per minute. Try sustaining each chord for four full beats at first, then see what guitar or keyboard rhythm patterns are suggested by the drums and play them both with and without the drum machine. If you don't have access to a drum machine, play or tap along with some of the recordings cited as examples until you get the "feel" of the grooves at different tempos. In any case, choose one combination of groove and tempo that most appeals to you, and use it as the basis for a complete song.

Sixteenth-Note Grooves

The other rhythmic subdivision most frequently heard on the radio today is the *sixteenth-note groove*. This groove, in which each beat is subdivided into four equal parts, is one you'll hear frequently in dance clubs. In addition, rock hits such as U2's "Mysterious Ways" and "I Still Haven't Found What I'm Looking For" and the Cranberries' "Linger" are also played with an underlying sixteenth-note subdivision. If you compare the Pet Shop Boys' 1988 version of "Always on my Mind" (co-written by Thompson, James, and Christopher) with Willie Nelson's, you'll clearly hear the difference between sixteenth- and eighth-note grooves.

The simplest and perhaps most obvious variation of the sixteenth-note groove is created by playing one of the simpler eighth-note kick and snare drum patterns we looked at earlier and having the high hat play four times for each beat instead of two. Producer Patrick Leonard used this technique on Madonna's "Open Your Heart," which she co-wrote with Gardner Cole and Peter Rafelson. Here is the basic drum groove from that song:

Notice that the kick and snare pattern is exactly the same as the one we examined from "Losing My Religion" on page 186, but the high hat is playing sixteenth notes instead of eighths, which gives the song an entirely different feeling.

Another frequently used variation of this rhythmic subdivision is the so-called "gallop" pattern, in which the second of the four sixteenth notes in every beat is omitted. Drummer/co-writer Jim Gordon used this pattern, illustrated below, to create the rhythmic foundation for Derek and the Dominos' "Layla," as did producers Giorgio Moroder and Pete Belotte on Donna Summer's two biggest hits, "Hot Stuff" and "Bad Girls":

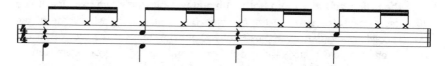

In both of the examples we have looked at so far, sixteenths are played on the high hat, but the kick and snare drums are limited to quarter and eighth notes. It's also possible, however, to have the bass drum play on a sixteenth-note subdivision. This gives us more opportunities for varying the kick drum pattern because there are sixteen possibilities for placement rather than eight. Let's examine, for instance, the drum groove from Des'ree's 1995 hit "You Gotta Be" (co-written with Ashley Ingram):

As you listen to this example, notice the additional drive created by the sixteenth note in the bass drum immediately before the second beat. If you program it on your drum machine making that note an eighth note and bringing it in a quarter beat earlier, you'll hear the difference created by including sixteenth notes in the bass as well as the high hat.

A sixteenth-note groove does not necessarily use percussion on all of the available sixteenth-note subdivisions. It's possible to create a more subtle version of this groove by merely placing one or two sixteenth notes somewhere in the measure. Listen to the drum pattern George Michael used in his 1988 number 1 hit "Father Figure":

This example is remarkable more for what it leaves out than what it adds. Notice that the only sixteenth note occurs in the "gallop" pattern on the first beat of the measure and that the high hat on the second, third, and fourth beats plays only eighth notes. Notice also the omission of the snare drum on the second beat, which has been found in all of the other patterns we have examined so far in this chapter, and the anticipation of the kick drum before the third beat. George Michael is a first-rate writer/producer who is as aware of the effect of drum programming and groove on his music as he is of melodies and chord progressions. If you're familiar with this song, you'll remember its unusual intimate quality. Michael's drum groove helped create prosody by underscoring that emotional feeling. If you slow the drum groove of "You Gotta Be" down to approximately the same tempo as that of "Father Figure" and try singing "Father Figure"'s words and melody against it, the subtle effect of Michael's understated sixteenth-note groove will become apparent.

ASSIGNMENT

Program the sixteenth-note grooves we have discussed on your drum machine and experiment with playing different combinations of chord progressions over them at various tempos as you did with eighth-note grooves (or play along with some of the recordings mentioned in this section). Then try capturing the sixteenth-note feeling using your guitar or keyboard alone. Choose one of the possibilities you develop and use it as the rhythmic basis for a complete song.

Triple-Meter Grooves

Thus far we have looked at the two most popular grooves in contemporary music, which subdivide each beat into two and four parts respectively. We're now going to examine a third type of groove, which, while not as common as the first two, still has been used as the rhythmic basis for a wide variety of successful songs in many different idioms. It subdivides each beat into *three* equal parts and is called *triple-meter groove.*

Triplet Groove

There are several distinct types of triple-meter grooves available. The first and perhaps easiest to understand is the so-called *triplet groove,* where all of the three subdivisions of each beat are played. We can find an example in Hugh Padgham's production of Melissa Etheridge's 1995 hit "I'm the Only One":

The first thing you may notice about this example is that it's written in 12/8 rather than 4/4 time (if you need to, refer back to the explanation on page 35 in Chapter 4). This is necessary to notate the three subdivisions of each beat without having to resort to using cumbersome triplet signs on each group of eighth notes. Other well-known songs built on a similar triplet groove include En Vogue's "Giving Him Something He Can Feel," Madonna's "True Blue," and most '50s style ballads such as Curtis Williams's "Earth Angel," which was originally recorded by both the Crew Cuts and the Penguins in 1955 and hit the charts again in a recording by the New Edition in 1986.

The Shuffle

A second type of triple-meter groove commonly found in contemporary music is the *shuffle,* in which the second of the three triplets in each beat is eliminated. Alan Jackson is one of the many country artists who have used this rhythmic pattern to build hits such as "Here in the Real World" (by Jackson and Mark Irwin) and "She's Got the Rhythm and I Got the Blues" (by Jackson and Randy Travis). This is the groove from "Here in the Real World":

Upon first glance, this groove looks exactly the same as that of "Losing My Religion," which we examined earlier. You'll notice, however, that in the upper left-hand corner there is a symbol indicating that two eighth notes equal a quarter note and an eighth note under a triplet sign. Shuffle grooves are commonly notated in this way for the sake of convenience, because there are really only two rhythmic attacks per beat, even though the first is twice as long as the second. In addition to country hits, a number of rock classics have been built on the shuffle as well, including Eric Clapton's unplugged version of "Layla" (which we discussed earlier) and Fleetwood Mac's "Don't Stop" (written by group member Christine McVie), which Bill Clinton used as the theme song of his 1992 presidential campaign.

The Swing Groove

We frequently find a third type of triple-meter groove, the *swing groove*, in jazz and country but rarely in pop or rock. In this style, the kick, snare drum, and high hat attacks are more irregular, but all notes played off the beat are the same "swing" (uneven) eighths found in the shuffle, the first eighth note lasting for two-thirds of the beat. Listen to Van Morrison's "Moondance" or the work of jazz-oriented artists such as Tony Bennett to get an idea of the sound of swing. A variation of this groove with a more regular kick and snare pattern has also been used in a style of country music known as "Texas Swing," from as far back as Bob Wills' 1939 recording of "San Antonio Rose" to contemporary hits like Chris LeDoux's duet with Garth Brooks, "Whatcha Gonna Do with A Cowboy" (by Brooks and Mark Sanders).

The Sixteenth-Note Shuffle

Until 1989, virtually every song was written to either an eighth-note, sixteenth-note, or triple-meter groove. In February of that year, however, Paula Abdul rocked the music world with her recording of Elliot Wolff's "Straight Up," which topped the pop and dance charts for three weeks. Though there was nothing extraordinary about the lyric, harmony, or melody of the song, it featured a different groove called the sixteenth-note shuffle, which later came to be referred to as "new jack swing." In this groove, the eighth notes are played "straight" (dividing the beat evenly in half) but the sixteenth notes are actually the first and third of a sixteenth-note triplet. Around the same time, Bobby Brown declared it was "My Prerogative" to use the groove as well, and within a year more than half the songs on the dance charts used new jack swing to create their underlying rhythmic foundation. An excellent example is Mariah Carey's "Someday" (co-written with Ben Margulies), which is built on this drum pattern:

The difference between this and the regular sixteenth-note groove is very subtle, and I strongly recommend listening to several examples to get the "feel" of it. A good way to grasp this difference is to compare the groove of Steve Winwood's Grammy-winning "Higher Love" (co-written with Will Jennings) with the one that producer Shep Pettibone used on the chorus of Madonna's 1992 remake of the Davenport-Cooley classic "Fever" (which charted for Peggy Lee 34 years earlier with an eighth-note swing groove). With the exception of the deleted sixteenth-note hi-hat at the end of the first beat, the added eighth-note kick drum at the end of the measure, and the symbol in the upper left-hand corner indicating that two sixteenth notes equal an eighth note and a sixteenth note under a triplet sign in "Fever," both grooves are written exactly alike:

Program these grooves on your drum machine and/or listen to the recordings from which they were taken. Because the kick, snare, and high-hat patterns are virtually identical, the difference you hear results solely from the "feel" of the sixteenth notes—evenly spaced (in "Higher Love") or "swung" (in "Fever").

In addition to dance hits such as "Straight Up" and "Fever," much of today's rap music such as Naughty by Nature's "Hip Hop Hooray" is built on the sixteenth-note shuffle. It can also be found in more mainstream pop songs such as Aaron Neville's "Don't Take Away My Heaven" (by Diane Warren) and Billy Joel's "River of Dreams," and even in country tunes such as Diamond Rio's 1995 hit "Night is Fallin' in My Heart" (by Dennis Linde).

ASSIGNMENT

Program the triplet, shuffle, and sixteenth-note shuffle grooves into your drum machine. As you did with the eighth- and sixteenth-note grooves, experiment with playing first a single chord against each one and then a series of chords. As before, work with the original recordings if no drum machine is available. Try to capture the feeling of each groove on your keyboard or guitar alone, then choose a variation that inspires you and develop it into a complete song.

Wrap-Up

In this chapter we've explored the various grooves used to create the rhythmic framework of a song. Whether you are an "outside" writer writing for a particular artist or a writer/artist aiming for a particular market, it's extremely important to listen to the radio and become familiar with the particular grooves and tempos commonly associated with the styles of music to which you are directing your writing.

Curtis Stone of Highway 101, one of my collaborators who was a staff writer at MCA Music in the mid-'80s, told me that sometimes when writers there were feeling a lack of inspiration they would go to the drum machine they all shared and jog their creativity by listening to some of the grooves that other writers had programmed. You can do this yourself by copying the grooves from some of your favorite songs on your drum machine and then experimenting with different melodies, harmonies, and even tempos to create your own original sound. If you have no access to a drum machine, just play along with any recording on your piano or guitar until you have captured the essence of the groove, then turn it off and apply the same rhythmic feeling to a different set of chords.

One final point about grooves: many songs that appear on the charts (particularly on the Dance charts) contain nothing more than simple, repetitive melodies played over very fascinating and elaborately produced grooves. While such "groove tunes" may get airplay for a brief amount of time or even become hits, they are generally quickly forgotten and never rerecorded. A thorough understanding of rhythm is most valuable when it is used not as a substitute for good harmonic and melodic writing, but rather as a strong, supportive foundation for inventive harmonies and exciting melodies. As songwriter/producer Michael Omartian (who has worked with Whitney Houston, Donna Summer, Amy Grant, and Vince Gill, among others) puts it, "I've played drums all my life and some of my hits like 'Tell Me I'm Not Dreaming' started out as drum patterns. But if I want to perpetuate the standard that I feel is important for songwriting, I can't rely on a drum machine at the expense of melodic and chordal content."

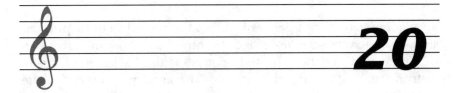

20

Arrangement and the Demo

Imagine you've finally completed that song you just *know* is going to be a hit. The melody is exciting and memorable, the chord progression is fresh and innovative, and it's got a terrific underlying groove that ties the other musical elements together perfectly. There's still one more step you need to take, however, before your work as a songwriter/composer is complete. If you're an "outside writer" whose primary objective is to have the song covered by an established recording artist, you must play it for publishers and producers who are in a position, if they agree it's a potential hit, to pitch it directly to the artist. If you're a writer/artist who's planning to use the tune to help get your own recording contract, you'll have to submit it to A&R (Artist & Repertoire) representatives at record labels who will decide whether or not to sign you. Even if you're an artist who *already has* a record deal, you still need to present the song to the record-buying public.

The form in which that presentation is made is known as the *arrangement*, which includes such considerations as choice of instruments that accompany the vocal, the specific role each instrument will play, background vocals, solos, introductions, and endings. The

195

arrangement does not generally affect the melody, chord progression, or basic verse-chorus-bridge *structure* of a tune (although a particular section may be repeated or used as the background for an instrumental solo at the discretion of the arranger), except in the case of the arranger's modulations we discussed in Chapter 11.

The Demo

To demonstrate your arrangement effectively, you'll need to create what is known as a *demo tape*. Even if you have a personal relationship with a publisher, producer, or A&R representative and can play the song for him or her live, a tape is necessary for your contact to present it to others involved in the decision-making process.

Years ago, home demos could be made relatively simply. Hit songwriter Alan O'Day landed his first Top 40 recording, Bobby Sherman's 1971 release "The Drum," with a 2-track demo that consisted of his playing the electric piano and singing the melody on one track and banging out the groove on the top of the piano on the other. In those days, once a professional recording of a song was secured, the producer would generally hire an arranger to assist with instrumentation, introductions, endings, etc., to create a finished master recording. Today's technological breakthroughs, however, have enabled the songwriter to gain access to enough equipment to simulate a complete master arrangement in his or her own living room, including realistic drum, bass, horn, and string sounds, as well as many of the additional synthesized and sampled sounds heard on contemporary radio.

Even if you don't have the economic means to set up a studio for yourself, there are now low-cost demo studios available in most major cities where you can easily and inexpensively gain access to the necessary equipment. In addition, if you own a personal computer and a keyboard with MIDI (Musical Instrument Digital Interface), you can purchase software that will enable you to digitally sequence many of the parts of your arrangement at home. You can then bring the disk with you into a professional studio and electronically interface with all the samplers, synthesizers, and sound-processing equipment available there.

As a result of this new technology, most of the people in the music industry whose job it is to find potential hit songs have become spoiled. While many of them (particularly those who work in country music) can still hear a great song with just a guitar/vocal or piano/vocal demo, chances are that, because all the other songs they listen to will most likely have full and complete arrangements, submitting a demo such as the one Alan O'Day presented over twenty years ago may result in a potential hit being overlooked.

Barry Kolsky, a publisher and songplugger in Los Angeles, has successfully used demos to secure recordings with a wide variety of artists including Tim McGraw, Gladys Knight, Huey Lewis, and Bette Midler. Here's what he has to say about submitting songs to the recording industry: "In my ten years of 'pitching songs' to artists and their handlers, I still find no consistency in the way tunes are chosen for a specific project. For that reason alone, the demo should be the best and most complete rendition of the song that you (the writer) can provide. As long as a song is well-written to begin with, a demo that's fully produced and 'radio ready' will be a big asset in helping to sell it."

We're now going to look at what it takes to create an arrangement that will give a demo the type of sound to which Kolsky was referring. We'll be focusing on the necessary components of such an arrangement, rather than on how to choose and notate parts for specific instruments such as bass, horns, or strings. If you're interested in a more detailed study of *that* aspect of arranging, I recommend both a good college-level course on the subject and the willingness to spend hours transcribing and analyzing recordings that you admire.

Instrumentation

The first decision you'll need to make when creating an arrangement for your demo is choosing the appropriate instruments. One of the most important factors in making this decision will be which market you are writing for. We'll discuss in depth the various *formats*, or styles of music played on the radio, in Chapter 21. For now, it's important only that you listen to recordings of the artists to whom you want to sell your material (or whose sound is similar to yours if you're a writer/artist) and be aware of the instrumentation idiomatic to their particular style.

Except for certain types of dance and R&B music (which we'll explore later), the heart of any arrangement consists of the lead singer's vocal and an instrument playing the chord progression. This instrument is usually the electric or acoustic guitar, the piano, or the "electronic keyboard," which includes analog and digital synthesizers, samplers, and various sound modules that can be accessed through a MIDI controller keyboard.

The *acoustic guitar* is the most common chordal instrument in country music. It can be picked, as in Tracy Byrd's 1996 CMA Song of the Year "The Keeper of the Stars" (by Lee, Mayo, and Staley), or strummed, as in Travis Tritt's self-penned "Here's A Quarter (Call Someone Who Cares)." It's also found in pop tunes such as George Michael's "Faith" and rock tunes such as Bon Jovi's "Wanted Dead or Alive" (co-written by Jon Bon Jovi and Ritchie Sambora), which uses a twelve-string guitar. The nylon-stringed classical guitar is sometimes used to add a Spanish flavor to songs such as Bryan Adams's 1995 no. 1 hit "Have You Ever Really Loved a Woman?" (co-written with Mutt Lange and Michael Kamen).

The *electric guitar* has been the primary chordal instrument of rock and roll since the days of Bill Haley and Chuck Berry in the '50s, and this tradition is carried on today by groups ranging from more mainstream rock bands such as U2 and REM to harder metal acts such as Queensryche and Metallica. The *acoustic piano* is used in a variety of idioms, ranging from contemporary country tunes such as Trisha Yearwood's "Walkaway Joe" (written by Vince Melamed and Greg Barnhill) to R&B/Pop by artists such as Anita Baker and James Ingram.

Electronic keyboards are by far the most popular chordal instruments in music today because of the diversity of sounds they can generate. It's even becoming quite common for an artist to play a basic rhythm track into a computer and then use the computer to drive any number of hi-tech samplers, synthesizers, and effects units that, in the hands of a skillful engineer/programmer, can create an almost infinite variety of sounds. In fact, as you'll discover if you have access to this equipment yourself, the sounds of these instruments can often suggest actual *writing* possibilities. Martin Page, who has had hits both as an artist (his "In the House of Stone and Light" hit number 1 on the adult contemporary charts in 1995) and as an outside songwriter of such tunes as Heart's "These Dreams" and Starship's "We Built This City", describes his experience: "I don't always go straight for the chords first. I may sit down at the synthesizer and find a sound that makes me feel like I'm seeing clouds or a storm, then I may run it through a board with reverb, hearing the echo returns and then feeding them into a delay, and hear the most incredible 3-D visual sounds. Finally, I'll put a melody and chords on top of that, and I'm creating a fresh, original sound that I wouldn't be otherwise. That's when I start to feel style."

Other instrumental considerations to be aware of include:

1. What instrument will provide the basic groove—drums, drum machine, or the chordal instrument itself without the use of any additional percussion?
2. What instrument will play the bass line—bass guitar, string bass, or synthesized/sampled keyboard bass?
3. What instruments will play the instrumental counter-melodies? (Synthesizers most commonly perform this function in pop or dance, the electric guitar in rock and roll, the saxophone in jazz and R&B, and the pedal steel guitar or fiddle in country music.)

Once these basic instrumentation decisions have been made, you're ready to begin to create your arrangement.

"Groove Up" Writing

An interesting system of musical composition known as *groove up* writing has become quite popular since the mid- to late '80s. In this style, choosing the instrumental textures and creating the arrangement are actually a part of the songwriting process. Rather than starting with chords and melody, writers using this technique *begin* by programming a drum pattern. They then build the musical track by putting a bass line and instrumental melodic lines and/or "stabs" (short chordal bursts) on top of the basic groove, before finally adding the vocal melody and lyrics.

Although it has been used throughout the history of pop, this style has become much more common in recent times, because new technology has made it possible for a songwriter to set the groove and layer the instruments in the privacy of his or her own studio without having to bring in other players. Writer/producer teams such as L. A. Reid and Babyface or Jimmy Jam and Terry Lewis, who have written and produced for a wide variety of recording artists ranging from Toni Braxton and Janet Jackson to Boyz II Men and George Michael, are among the contemporary masters of this style, as are "industrial" rock groups such as Nine Inch Nails. In addition, many rock tunes from the Beatles' "Come Together" to the Red Hot Chili Peppers' "Give it Away" have their origins in "groove up" writing. It is also the cornerstone on which virtually all the background tracks for today's rap music are built.

An excellent example of this type of writing can be found in Janet Jackson's first hit, "What Have You Done for Me Lately" (co-written with producers Jam and Lewis). The song begins with the simplest possible groove, using only a kick drum on the first and third beats of each measure and a highly processed snare drum sound on two and four. To that, the producers add the following bass line:

Notice that in this song, the sixteenth-note groove is created not by the drum machine (which plays only quarter notes) but rather by the *bass line* with its sixteenth-note anticipation of the fourth beat in each measure and additional sixteenth note at the end of every other measure. The verse melody is sung over this drum and bass groove until the following figure is played on the synthesizer, with the chordal stab landing on the downbeat of the chorus:

This sequence of notes, with several variations, continues throughout the chorus in a call and response pattern with the lead vocal (that is, it is played in the spaces between the vocal phrases). While you could say that the harmonic accompaniment of the verse and the chorus consists primarily of an E♭-minor chord, there is a vast difference between the groove bass lines and synthesizer counterlines and stabs used in this "groove up" style and merely having a chordal instrument block out an E♭-minor triad with bass accompaniment.

"What Have You Done for Me Lately," while an excellent illustration of solid "groove up" writing, is also one of the simpler examples of this style. Songs such as Phil Collins' number 1 hit "Sussudio" and C+C Music Factory's "Gonna Make You Sweat (Everybody Dance Now)" use more complex drum patterns to which are added all sorts of synthesizer lines and counterlines, guitar riffs, and even full horn sections. "Groove up" writing is very popular in contemporary dance, R&B, and Top 40/Pop. If it appeals to you, some practice and experimentation are likely to yield very interesting and satisfying results.

ASSIGNMENT

If you have the equipment available, create an original drum pattern on your drum machine, either by starting from scratch (if you're comfortable with drum programming) or using a variation of one of the patterns we diagramed in Chapter 19. Then, on your keyboard, bass, or guitar, experiment until you have come up with a fresh, original bass line that "locks in" with that groove. Next, record the drums and bass on either your sequencer or one of the channels of a multitrack tape machine. Try playing either stabs or counterlines against it with your keyboard or guitar, like the one in the example from "What Have You Done for Me Lately," until you've created a drum/bass/keyboard (guitar) pattern that you like. Then try putting a melody on top of that, perhaps repeating one motif with variations, until you've developed an interesting hook chorus.

Instrumental Hooks

In terms of albums sold and number 1 records, the Beatles are by far the most popular rock band of all time. Among the many reasons for their great success were the distinctive *instrumental hooks*, usually played by lead guitarist George Harrison, that are in many cases more easily remembered than the actual melodies of their songs. Think of the lead guitar lines associated with classics such as "Day Tripper," "And I Love Her," and "Birthday" (from the *White Album*), and the lasting influence of these licks, some of them written more than thirty years ago, will be apparent.

Instrumental hooks, while not a necessary part of an arrangement, can contribute immeasurably to making a song more memorable. They can be played on almost any instrument. Tom Snow, for example, built the music for his hit "Let's Hear It for the Boy" (with lyrics by Dean Pitchford) on this distinctive bass line:

While bass lines such as this appear mostly in pop and R&B, guitar is perhaps *the* classic instrument for instrumental hooks in rock and roll. From Cream's "Sunshine of Your Love" and the Rolling Stones' "Satisfaction" to contemporary hits such as Dire Straits' "Money for Nothing" and the Spin Doctors' "Jimmy Olsen's Blues," the guitar riff has cemented the sound of many favorite rock and roll tunes into listeners' minds. Still, the use of the guitar to play instrumental hooks is not by any means limited to rock. Smokey Robinson's classic "My Girl" (co-written with R. White), which was a number 1 hit for The Temptations and later recorded by Hall & Oates and Suave, among others, and Dwight Yoakum's "Fast as You" are among the many examples of R&B and country songs that feature distinctive musical figures played on the electric guitar.

Other instruments that have been used to create instrumental hooks include the saxophone (George Michael and Wham!'s "Careless Whispers"), the harmonica (Clint Black's "Put Yourself in My Shoes"), the piano (Bruce Hornsby's "The Way It Is"), and of course synthesizers and samplers. If you listen to this passage played by sampled strings, Annie Lennox's 1992 hit "Walking on Broken Glass" will come immediately to mind:

Placement of Instrumental Hooks

Instrumental hooks are generally used in three different ways. Some of them are only played on introductions or between sections of a song, such as the harmonica lick from "Put Yourself in My Shoes" or this opening piano riff from "The Way It Is":

If an instrumental hook is performed on bass or a chordal instrument, like the sampled string part from "Walking on Broken Glass" or the bass line from "Let's Hear It for the Boy," it is often played underneath the vocal melody as well as during the introduction.

A third way to incorporate instrumental hooks is to insert them between the vocal lines, like the synth figure in "What Have You Done for Me Lately" or the guitar lick in "Birthday." These licks "bracket" the vocals; that is, they begin after one vocal phrase and end before the next one starts, and are sometimes called *counter-melodies.* The piano figure from "The Way It Is," illustrated below, which begins the chorus and is repeated after each of the first three vocal phrases, is a good example of this:

Again, while it isn't *necessary* to have an instrumental hook in an arrangement, a distinctive introductory musical phrase or an interesting counterline during the chorus definitely adds another dimension to a song.

Intros and Endings

There is an old musical saying that "The hardest thing in the world is to start an orchestra, and the next hardest thing is to stop it." While we're not dealing with complete orchestras in a demo, the impression made by the introduction and ending can be crucial to the overall effect of an arrangement.

Intros on demos should generally be short (no more than eight bars), unless they are live performances of tunes written by members of a band that are being used to showcase the overall sound of the group as well as the songs. If you have an instrumental hook in your arrangement, the introduction is probably the best place to present it so that it sounds familiar when it recurs later on. If there is no instrumental hook, you might have a lead instrument play or paraphrase the melody of either the verse or the chorus. If the tune is written from the groove up, you may want to use the introduction to recreate the way it was developed, starting with the drums and then gradually adding bass, synthesizer, and other instruments. In any case, the most important thing to keep in mind is that the purpose of the introduction is to set the stage for the song itself. A great intro is only great if it fulfills that function.

Endings are generally of two types: the hard ending and the fade ending. The *hard ending* recreates the effect of a live performance where everyone stops together, usually with the singer sustaining a whole note and the band sustaining a I (or Im) chord. This is the most common type of ending on ballads, songs with an A-A-B-A form, and demos of live bands. A *fade ending* is created by gradually reducing the volume of a song from the mixing console while the music continues. It is used frequently on mid- and uptempo verse-chorus songs where the hook in the chorus is repeated over and over through the fade. If there is a distinctive instrumental figure, it may also be repeated, either alone or along with the lyric/melodic hook. As you listen to more and more songs on the radio with an ear for arrangement, your skill as an arranger will grow and you'll become both more professional and more creative in deciding which type of ending is most appropriate for each of *your* songs.

The Vocal

As we mentioned in Chapter 13, the lead vocal is the part of a song to which the listener pays the most attention. It is therefore the most important part of your demo and arrangement. I like to think of a song as a beautiful ring, with the lead vocal as the precious stone in the center and everything else as the setting. Exciting grooves, instrumental hook licks, interesting synthesizer sounds, and "hip" intros and endings will all be wasted unless the vocal is clear, audible, and in tune.

If you are a writer/artist, be sure to allow yourself enough time in the studio to get a vocal "take" that is as close to perfect as possible. If you are not a professional vocalist or performer yourself, you should seriously consider having someone else sing on your demo. Carla Berkowitz, Director of Writer/Catalog Development for EMI Music Publishing, who has secured recordings with a variety of artists including Cher, Joe Cocker, Anita Baker, and James Ingram, has this to say about the subject: "A good singer is totally necessary. I consider myself being able to hear a good song no matter what the production on the demo, but a poor vocal gets so much in the way, it's nearly impossible. It's like a big sore thumb sticking out that you just can't get past. If someone else can do a better job singing it than you, step back and let them do it. I know many writers who insist on singing their own demos, and that's the main reason they're not getting cuts, because they add their own inflection and style and that interferes with the song."

Remember, no matter how much it "feels right" when you sing your song, it will feel even better when you get that publishing or recording contract, so make sure you present it with the absolute best vocal possible.

Background Vocals

In addition to the lead vocalist singing the melody, singers are frequently used in arrangements to perform *background vocals*, which fall into three categories. In the first, *harmony vocals*, the background singers sing the words of a particular part of the tune (most commonly the hook) in harmony with the lead vocalist. For example, at the beginning of the chorus of the Eagles' "Best of My Love" (co-written by John David Souther and group members Don Henley and Glenn Frey, and also recorded by Brooks and Dunn), the lead singer sings this melody:

At the same time, the background vocalists, whose overall sound is lower in the *mix* (relative volumes and placements of the different parts of an arrangement in the final recording), are singing these harmony lines:

After two verses and a chorus, the bridge begins on a IVm7 chord with the lyrics, "I'm goin' back in time and it's a sweet dream." In that section we hear a second common type of background vocals, in which a number of voices, usually singing "ooo's" (as in "Best of My Love"), "oh's," or "ah's", quietly sustain the notes of the chord being played by the keyboard or guitar. This is known as a *vocal pad* and is a technique found in all styles of music, from country to pop to R&B.

Sometimes background vocals will work in a third, *call and response* pattern, bracketing the lead vocal in the same way as the instrumental licks we discussed earlier. One of the best-known examples of this occurs in Aretha Franklin's hit version of Otis Redding's "Respect," where the background singers singing "Just a little bit," "Re-re-re-re-spect," and "Sock it to me" are as integral a part of the performance as Aretha's lead vocal.

It's just as important to choose quality background vocalists for your demo as it is to choose a good lead singer. Very often the lead vocalist can also perform all the background parts by singing each one separately on a different track (known as multitracking). However, not all singers are skilled in this particular art. Many of them are capable of giving a very high-quality, emotional rendering of the message of a song but have difficulty harmonizing with themselves. Again, whether the background vocals are sung by you, your lead vocalist, or additional singers you bring in for that purpose, the most important thing is that they be clear and in tune.

Choose half-a-dozen songs that are currently being played on the radio in the style(s) in which you are primarily interested in writing (feel free to include some of the ones you selected for the structural analysis exercise in Chapter 2). Either tape them from the radio or purchase the recording, then listen to them closely and ask yourself the following questions:

1. What is the primary chordal instrument used in the song?
2. Is the percussion provided by a live drummer, a drum machine/sequencer, or a combination of the two?
3. Does the song sound as if it were written/arranged from the groove up or in a more traditional fashion?
4. What instrumental hooks or countermelodies (if any) are there? Where do they occur? What instrument plays them?
5. What type of intro and ending is used?
6. Are there background vocals, and if so, are they harmonies, pads, or call and response?

After you have written down the answers to these questions for each of the songs, see if there are any general trends in the type(s) of music you want to compose. I strongly recommend repeating this exercise every six months, or every time you attempt to write in a new style.

Wrap-Up

In this chapter we've looked at the various possibilities for expanding the basic melody, harmony, and groove of a song into a complete arrangement to be used in the demo you present to the industry. We've discussed many of the important aspects of that arrangement, including instrumentation, bass lines, instrumental hooks, intros, endings, and lead and background vocals.

However, the most important thing to keep in mind is that a great arrangement can only enhance a well-written song and make it more attractive; it cannot "save" a bad song. A great song will stand up to any arrangement and remain a great song.

For example, "You Keep Me Hangin' On," by the hit writing team of Holland/Dozier/Holland, has been on the *Billboard* Top 10 three times. The first release by the Supremes in 1966 was arranged in the Motown style that was so popular during that era. Two years later, the rock band Vanilla Fudge recorded a completely different version of the tune, which was nearly forty beats per minute slower than the original and featured the sustained Hammond organ and fuzz-tone guitar sounds characteristic of their style. The song charted again in 1987 with Kim Wilde's synth/pop arrangement, which restored its original tempo and featured sequenced drums and repeated sixteenth-note synthesizer figures. The success of all three versions clearly shows that the basic melody, harmony, and lyrics of "You Keep Me Hangin' On" make it a first-rate song no matter what the arrangement.

We've also spent some time in this chapter discussing the demo tape itself. I've deliberately avoided an extensive discussion of the multitrack tape recorders, mixing boards, and sound-processing equipment essential to creating a quality demo. Suffice it is to say that if you're doing your recording in a professional studio, an engineer will generally be available to handle those considerations. If you're planning to set up your own studio at home, be certain you engage a good engineer as a consultant to help you get started before attempting to track and mix your own recordings.

The bottom line for demos in today's music industry can best be summed up in the words of Bob Margouleff, Grammy-winning record producer and engineer who has worked with artists ranging from Stevie Wonder and Wilson Pickett to Seal and Sheryl Crow: "A demo can be simple, but it should have all the essential countermelody ideas and background vocal spaces. It should basically reflect the style of the song, and the basic song form should be well defined. I've recorded songs I originally heard as a piano/vocal, but in general the more literate and full-sounding the demo, the better chance you have of hooking somebody with the song."

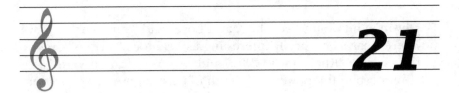

21

Collaboration and the Marketplace

Now that we've examined how to create an arrangement for a song and present it in the form of a demo, our inquiry into writing music for hit songs is virtually complete. Only two elements remain to be discussed: *writing the lyric* and *getting the song recorded*. While it's beyond the scope of this book to go into either of these subjects in detail, I wanted to briefly touch on a few key points in each area to help you start on the path to both finding the appropriate words for your music and having the songs that result reach the widest possible audience.

Finding the Right Lyric

Popular songwriting is a unique art form. While there have been many beautiful and memorable melodies and chord progressions written in the genre through the years, the most outstanding examples still pale in comparison *musically* with the work of classical masters such as Bach, Beethoven, Debussy, and Stravinsky. Even George

209

Gershwin's "hits," such as "The Man I Love" and "Summertime," are nowhere near as musically interesting as his more "serious" orchestral pieces like "Rhapsody in Blue" and "An American in Paris."

Yet despite the power and depth of classical music, you seldom hear people walking down the street humming the melody of a concerto. Nor do you hear them make comments such as "I get so moved when I hear that symphony because it reminds me of the summer when I met my first love." The reason for this is simple: classical orchestral music has no *lyrics* accompanying the melody. Our first response to pure music is generally an emotional or right brain response, whereas our first response to words, since the meaning of their sounds must be translated for them to make sense, is generally an intellectual or left brain response. Instrumental music, therefore, though it touches us emotionally, leaves our minds free to wander. The unique combination of music *and* lyrics, particularly if the prosody is strong (see Chapter 3), has a deeper impact because it hits us both intellectually and emotionally with the same message.

Although it's true that, as the hit songwriter Barry Mann has said, "If you have a great melody, you have a lot of the problem of having a hit solved," it's also true that to finish the job you need to be able to either write a great lyric or work with a great lyricist, as Mann does with his wife and longtime collaborator, Cynthia Weil. Although some very successful writers such as Billy Joel, Sting, and Diane Warren are as gifted with the verbal phrase as they are with the musical phrase, many other fine composers such as Elton John, David Foster, and Burt Bacharach call upon talented lyricists like Bernie Taupin, Linda Thompson, and Carole Bayer Sager to handle that part of the job. Still others such as Carole King, Steve Winwood, and Clint Black have both written alone and collaborated with lyricists at various stages of their careers.

Should You Collaborate?

I'm aware that some of you reading this book are *primarily* lyricists who want to get an equally solid grounding in the musical aspect of pop songwriting. For those of you who don't fall into this category, the most important criterion for choosing whether to work with a lyricist/collaborator is simply this: are *you* capable of writing words that will turn your melodic/harmonic/rhythmic compositions into hit songs? Like the question we raised in Chapter 20 regarding whether you should perform the vocals on your own demos, this is often an extremely difficult decision to make by yourself. For that reason, I suggest submitting demos of songs for which you have written both words and music to publishers and other people in the industry to get their reactions. If you're constantly being told, "These tunes are musically strong but lyrically weak," perhaps it would be a good idea to get an experienced co-writer to either write the words for you or assist you in crafting your own concepts and story lines into top-quality lyrics.

Although there's a tendency for composers to feel that "anyone who talks can write lyrics," this is not an accurate assessment. Given that you've taken the time to read this book through, I've no doubt that you're serious about your music writing. The fact is that many lyricists out there are just as serious about *their* craft and have spent the same number of hours working with the English language as you have studying scales, chords, and grooves. This is certainly not meant to discourage you from writing your own lyrics. I'm only suggesting that, before you make a final decision to be a completely self-contained writer, you examine the possibilities for collaboration.

Types of Collaboration

From the turn of the century through the mid-'60s, the most common form of collaboration was to divide the creation of a song along strict musical/lyrical lines, the composer providing the melodies and harmonies and the lyricist the words. From Rodgers and Hammerstein through Elton John and Bernie Taupin, this traditional division of labor has produced some of the best-known and most respected songs in the history of popular music.

There are basically two ways to collaborate with a lyricist in this style. Most hit lyric writers, such as Cynthia Weil ("Somewhere Out There," "He's So Shy") and Ron Miller ("For Once in My Life," "I've Never Been to Me"), prefer to match their lyrics to a completed music track. Others, such as Bernie Taupin (lyricist for all of Elton John's early recordings in addition to more recent hits, such as Heart's "These Dreams" and Starship's "We Built This City"), prefer to finish the lyric first and have the music written later. In either case, once both parts have been completed separately, the two writers will generally meet and iron out some of the details before declaring the product ready to market.

Writing Together

If you examine today's best-selling songs, whether Top 40, country, or R&B, you'll notice that well over 75 percent of them credit more than one songwriter. If you exclude self-contained acts such as Phil Collins, Mary Chapin-Carpenter, and Prince, that figure generally runs above 90 percent. In most of these contemporary collaborations, each writer has skills in both music and lyric writing, yet they choose to combine their talents for several reasons.

First, collaborating with a partner is a good way to get feedback and critique on a song *as* you're writing it. My own experience has shown that when I come up with a "brilliant" melodic, harmonic, or lyric idea only to have my writing partner say something like, "Well, why don't we put it aside for a moment and see if we can go for something else," the perspective of several days or weeks usually shows my partner to have been correct in his or her estimation. Other times, the exact opposite will happen. Either my partner or I will throw out a musical or lyric idea that we're not especially excited or enthusiastic about and the other will say, "No, that's great. Look what we can expand it into." I have personally found that such a give-and-take process produces far more interesting results than either my partner or I would have come up with on our own.

Another reason for co-writing is to find someone whose strengths and weaknesses complement your own. For example, if you are most proficient at writing grooves and melodic lines, look for a collaborator whose strong points are chord changes and lyrics. Billy Steinberg and Tom Kelly, who have written hits for Madonna, Heart, Cyndi Lauper, and Whitney Houston among others, are an excellent example of a writing team that works together this way. As Kelly says about his partner, "What I'm good at, he's not. What he's good at, I'm not."

A third reason for working with a partner is that, in practical terms, the more people there are writing a song, the more possible connections there are for getting it recorded. Furthermore, if your collaborators are also vocalists, arrangers, engineers, or studio musicians and you have built a solid relationship with them, they may someday be involved in a project and in a position to help place not only the songs that you have written together, but perhaps some of your other material as well.

A final benefit of collaboration is suggested by Jody Williams, President of MCA Music Publishing in Nashville and former Vice President of Writer/Publisher Relations at BMI: "Nashville is the co-writing capital of the world, and there are many reasons why writers here collaborate. It's easier, it's more fun, and you meet some really wonderful friends. But I ultimately think the best thing about co-writing is that it teaches you how to get better at critiquing your own work. Writing with others and listening to the comments that come from them can teach you things that will improve the quality of your songs even when you're writing on your own."

Remember, there are no hard-and-fast rules about collaboration, any more than there are about music or lyric writing. The bottom line is, whether your goals are artistic, commercial, or a combination of the two, experiment with different possibilities and follow the path that produces the most successful results.

ASSIGNMENT

Choose a well-known song whose lyric you particularly admire. Write out the words line by line, and then compose your own music to them. Although the lyric may dictate the melodic phrasing, you will find you have a wide variety of choices in terms of harmony, melodic pitch, and rhythmic groove. If you feel particularly adventurous, try selecting a lyric from a song in a less familiar style (for example, an R&B lyric if you are primarily a country writer, or a mainstream pop lyric if you usually write rock and roll), and see if it's possible to give it an effective musical treatment in *your* style.

Marketing Your Songs

In the course of writing this book I asked several very successful song-writers why they write songs. Their answers were remarkably similar and can be summarized as follows: "To express myself artistically and communicate to others in a way that makes a difference." It's only possible to have that kind of impact on a wide audience when that audience *hears* your songs. No matter how exciting your music or poignant your lyric, if it never gets beyond your living room, it has not fulfilled a major part of its purpose. In that sense, marketing your material can actually be considered a natural extension of the writing process.

Making Contacts

Unless your brother-in-law is a close personal friend of Whitney Houston or Garth Brooks, you're going to be facing the problem of presenting your songs through more traditional channels: publishers, producers, and A&R representatives. The majority of the people in these positions will not accept unsolicited material from beginning writers. Therefore, the most important part of marketing your songs is building *relationships* with people in the business. The best way to begin that process is by making contact with anyone in the music industry you can, whether it's an attorney, engineer, studio musician, small independent publisher, or perhaps even the secretary of a record company executive.

When making this initial contact, whether in person or by mail, the key to a successful first impression is being professional in your speaking. Every vocation, from auto mechanic to brain surgeon, has specific terminology that knowledgeable practitioners use to discuss their work. Just as it would be hard to get a job working on cars if your interview with the shop boss showed that you didn't know the difference between a distributor and a carburetor, it's equally diffi-cult to get someone in the music industry to even take the time to lis-ten to your songs if you don't speak their language.

One good way to build your knowledge of this language, as well as of current trends in the business, is to join songwriting organiza-tions like NAS (the National Academy of Songwriters) or NSAI (Nashville Songwriters Association International). Another is to read *Billboard* magazine regularly. Its subscribers include virtually every major record label and publishing company, and its weekly reports and charts are the industry standard. If you can't obtain it at your local newsstand, I strongly recommend subscribing or splitting a sub-scription with a songwriting friend if the high annual cost is prohib-itive for you.

Formats

One of the first things you'll notice as you look through the table of contents in *Billboard* is an extensive list of music charts. Each of these charts lists the current top-selling songs in the United States in vari-ous formats or styles of music (there is a full-page listing the best sell-ers in major international markets as well). These formats are very important to us as writers, because each radio station generally tends to limit its playlist to a particular format, and radio exposure is *the* most effective way to market a new artist or a new song by an estab-lished artist.

The four formats currently most popular are Top 40/Pop (the so-called "Hot 100"), Country, R&B (also known as Black or Urban music), and Adult Contemporary. In addition, many radio stations have what is known as an AOR (album-oriented rock) format where individual hits are often less important to record sales than a band's overall sound and image. (Check the Rock Tracks and Pop *Album* charts to keep up with music in this style.)

While it's not necessary or even desirable to write songs that sound like the current hottest sellers, it's still important to be aware of the trends in these areas so that your marketing strategy will be appropriate. For example, if you had written a song in the mid-'80s with lyrics that dealt with a current controversial issue, it would have been a good idea to go into an L.A. publisher's office with a demo that had a contemporary arrangement, saying, "This song has as good a chance to crack the Top 40 as Suzanne Vega's 'Luka' or Bruce Hornsby's 'The Way It Is,'" rather than walking in with a guitar/vocal demo proclaiming, "I think this could be a folk hit!" In the mid-'90s, your best bet might be bringing it to Nashville where such issue-oriented songs as John Anderson's "Seminole Wind" and Gretchen Peters' "Independence Day" (which won the 1995 Country Music Association Song of the Year award as recorded by Martina McBride) have been finding success.

Songs do not necessarily have to fit into one of the four most popular categories, however, to reach a wide audience. Many other specialized formats, including dance, gospel, jazz, reggae, New Age, Latin, children's music, and even musical theater, have their own production and distribution channels. The important thing to remember is that, no matter what style or format you write in, make certain you do your homework and thoroughly research the current trends in that idiom. That way, when you make the initial presentation of your material to a publisher, producer, or A&R person, you'll come across as a writer or writer/artist who is a knowledgeable as well as talented player in the music industry, rather than someone who is outside the game entirely.

Wrap-Up

Now that we've explored combining music with lyrics, collaborating, and effectively presenting your work to the industry, our discussion of writing music for hit songs is complete. After working through this book, you should have a thorough understanding of contemporary song forms as well as a sense of how to use prosody and contrast effectively. You should be familiar with both the basic chords and chord progressions of pop harmony and advanced techniques such as the use of inversions, extensions, and modulation. You should be able to effectively select both the pitches and rhythms of your melodies, taking into account good phrasing and motivic development. Finally, you should be comfortable writing in minor as well as major keys and have a solid understanding of groove and arrangement.

All of this information, however, does not by any stretch of the imagination guarantee that you will be able to write songs that get published and recorded. The point we have reached is not an end but rather a beginning. What you *should* be able to do by now is write and/or co-write songs that will let the music-industry professionals to whom you submit them know that you are a writer to be taken seriously. As you begin to get more deeply involved in the music *business* and develop relationships with publishers, producers, and A&R representatives, you'll find that your real learning takes place when your songs are *rejected* by these professionals, and they give you suggestions as to what they feel needs to be changed. This feedback, combined with the theoretical background you have gained from reading this book and a willingness to constantly rewrite and improve your work, will be the key to your ultimate success.

All of us started out as songwriters because we had some way in which we wanted to move others, whether it was to make them laugh, cry, reflect, or just get up and dance. You can bring that vision into reality if you're willing to constantly work on developing and perfecting your craft, both through classes and books such as this one and through applying feedback received from the industry.

Hit songwriter Tom Snow, several of whose songs we have examined in detail, summed it up best when he told me, "Songwriting is about ten percent inspiration and ninety percent craft. If it was only inspiration, I wouldn't have any hits because my expression would go so far afield that what I would be writing would be unrecordable. Inspiration is where it all begins, but it usually lasts a very small amount of time, and then the rest is hard work."

It is my most sincere hope that this book will be of assistance to you in doing that work, and that it will pay off by having *your* music heard and appreciated by millions of people.

Appendix

Chapter 4

EXERCISE 4–1

EXERCISE 4–1 (*continued*)

Chapter 5

EXERCISE 5–1

Major Scales

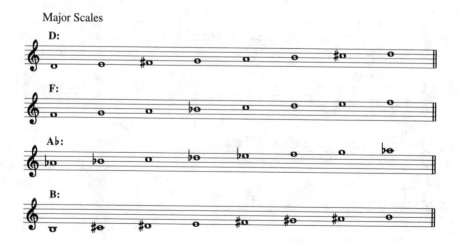

EXERCISE 5–2

Major Scales II

EXERCISE 5–3

Intervals

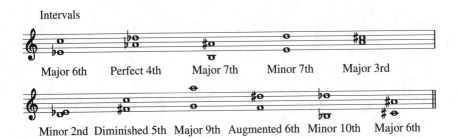

Major 6th   Perfect 4th   Major 7th   Minor 7th   Major 3rd

Minor 2nd Diminished 5th Major 9th Augmented 6th Minor 10th   Major 6th

Chapter 6

EXERCISE 6–1

"Featured Fourteen" Chords

EXERCISE 6–1 (*continued*)

Chapter 7

E<small>XERCISE</small> 7–1

Diatonic Triads

E<small>XERCISE</small> 7–1 (*continued*)

Diatonic Sevenths

E♭: Imaj7   IIm7   IIIm7   IVmaj7   V7   VIm7   VIIm7(♭5)

E♭maj7   Fm7   Gm7   A♭maj7   B♭7   Cm7   Dm7(♭5)

F: Imaj7   IIm7   IIIm7   IVmaj7   V7   VIm7   VIIm7(♭5)

Fmaj7   Gm7   Am7   B♭maj7   C7   Dm7   Em7(♭5)

G♭: Imaj7   IIm7   IIIm7   IVmaj7   V7   VIm7   VIIm7(♭5)

G♭maj7   A♭m7   B♭m7   C♭maj7   D♭7   E♭m7   Fm7(♭5)

G: Imaj7   IIm7   IIIm7   IVmaj7   V7   VIm7   VIIm7(♭5)

Gmaj7   Am7   Bm7   Cmaj7   D7   Em7   F♯m7(♭5)

A♭: Imaj7   IIm7   IIIm7   IVmaj7   V7   VIm7   VIIm7(♭5)

A♭maj7   B♭m7   Cm7   D♭maj7   E♭7   Fm7   Gm7(♭5)

E<small>XERCISE</small> 7–2

The Dance

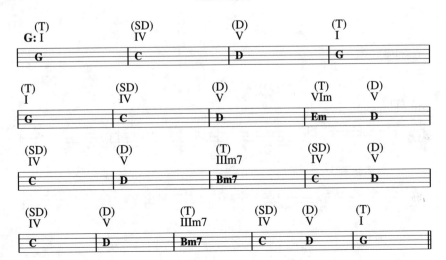

(T)   (SD)   (D)   (T)
G: I   IV   V   I

G   C   D   G

(T)   (SD)   (D)   (T)   (D)
I   IV   V   VIm   V

G   C   D   Em   D

(SD)   (D)   (T)   (SD)   (D)
IV   V   IIIm7   IV   V

C   D   Bm7   C   D

(SD)   (D)   (T)   (SD)   (D)   (T)
IV   V   IIIm7   IV   V   I

C   D   Bm7   C   D   G

Chapter 8

EXERCISE 8–1

V7sus4 Chords

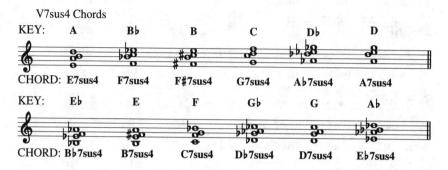

EXERCISE 8–2

♭VII and ♭VIImaj7 Chords

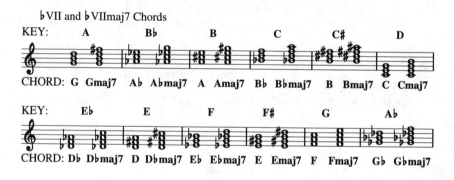

EXERCISE 8–3

What A Feeling

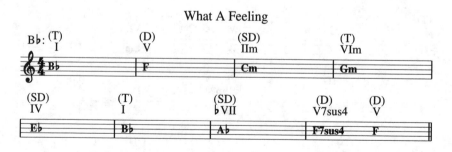

Chapter 9

EXERCISE 9–1

Secondary Dominants

Key of A:

V7 of II	V7 of III	V7 of IV	V7 of V	V7 of VI
(target chord: Bm or IIm)	(target chord: C#m or IIIm)	(target chord: D or IV)	(target chord: E or V)	(target chord: F#m or VIm)
F#7	G#7	A7	B7	C#7

Key of Bb:

V7 of II	V7 of III	V7 of IV	V7 of V	V7 of VI
(target chord: Cm or IIm)	(target chord: Dm or IIIm)	(target chord: Eb or IV)	(target chord: F or V)	(target chord: Gm or VIm)
G7	A7	Bb7	C7	D7

Key of D:

V7 of II	V7 of III	V7 of IV	V7 of V	V7 of VI
(target chord: Em or IIm)	(target chord: F#m or IIIm)	(target chord: G or IV)	(target chord: A or V)	(target chord: Bm or VIm)
B7	C#7	D7	E7	F#7

Key of Eb:

V7 of II	V7 of III	V7 of IV	V7 of V	V7 of VI
(target chord: Fm or IIm)	(target chord: Gm or IIIm)	(target chord: Ab or IV)	(target chord: Bb or V)	(target chord: Cm or VIm)
C7	D7	Eb7	F7	G7

Key of F:

V7 of II	V7 of III	V7 of IV	V7 of V	V7 of VI
(target chord: Gm or IIm)	(target chord: Am or IIIm)	(target chord: Bb or IV)	(target chord: C or V)	(target chord: Dm or VIm)
D7	E7	F7	G7	A7

Key of G:

V7 of II	V7 of III	V7 of IV	V7 of V	V7 of VI
(target chord: Am or IIm)	(target chord: Bm or IIIm)	(target chord: C or IV)	(target chord: D or V)	(target chord: Em or VIm)
E7	F#7	G7	A7	B7

EXERCISE 9–2

The Longest Time

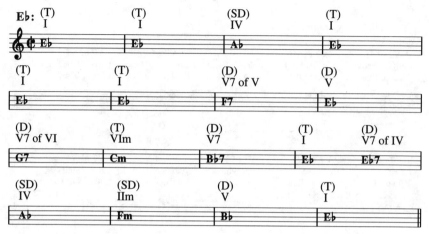

$E\flat$:
(T) I	(T) I	(SD) IV	(T) I
$E\flat$	$E\flat$	$A\flat$	$E\flat$

(T) I	(T) I	(D) V7 of V	(D) V
$E\flat$	$E\flat$	F7	$E\flat$

(D) V7 of VI	(T) VIm	(D) V7	(T) I	(D) V7 of IV
G7	Cm	$B\flat$7	$E\flat$	$E\flat$7

(SD) IV	(SD) IIm	(D) V	(T) I
$A\flat$	Fm	$B\flat$	$E\flat$

That's What Friends Are For

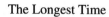

$E\flat$:
(T) I	(T) Imaj7	(SD) $\flat$VII	(D) V7 of II	(see chapter 18) IVm6
$E\flat$	$E\flat$maj7	$D\flat$	C7	$A\flat$m6/$C\flat$

Chapter 10

EXERCISE 10–1

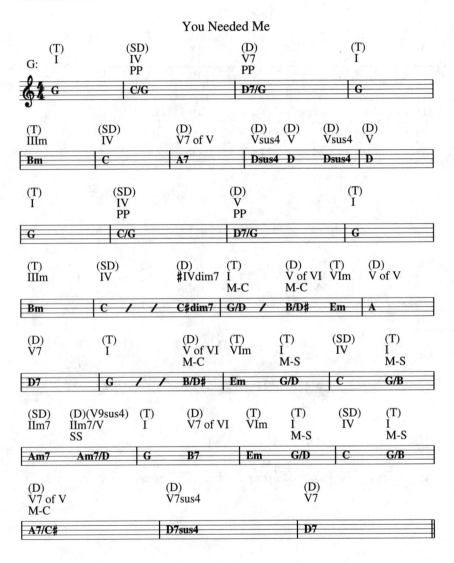

You Needed Me

Chapter 11

EXERCISE 11–1

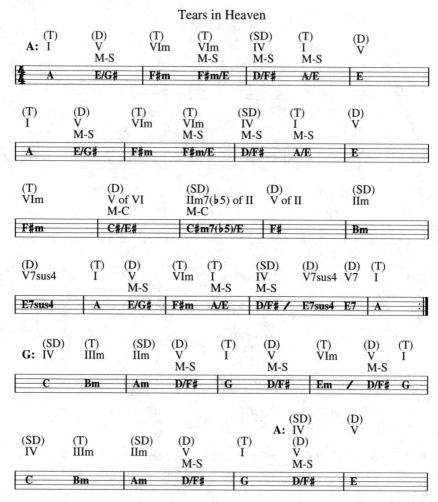

Tears in Heaven

Chapter 12

EXERCISE 12–1

Extensions and Alterations

Chapter 15

EXERCISE 15–1

Motivic Development
Addition

Subtraction

Pitch Variation

Pitch and Melodic Contour Variation

Variation in Melodic Rhythm

Pitch and Rhythm Variation

Chapter 16

EXERCISE 16–1

Aeolian Scales

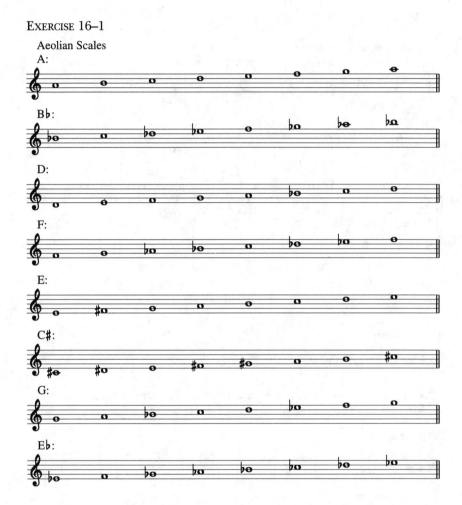

EXERCISE 16-2

Dorian Scales

EXERCISE 16–3

Blues Scales

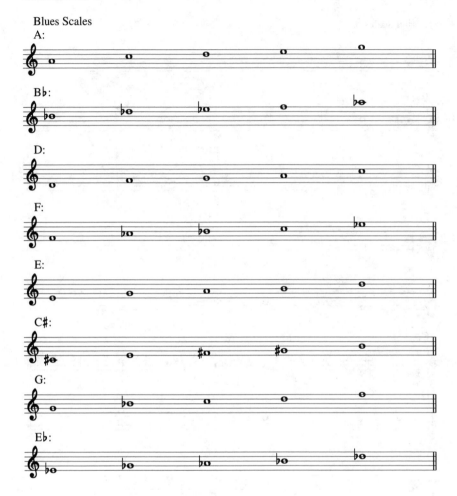

EXERCISE 16–4

Harmonic Minor Scales

Melodic Minor Scales

EXERCISE 16–4 (*continued*)

Phrygian Scales

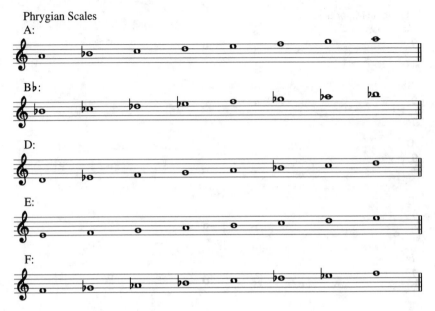

Chapter 17

EXERCISE 17–1

Diatonic Chords in Aeolian

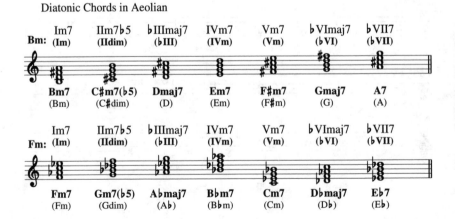

EXERCISE 17–2

Diatonic Chords in Dorian

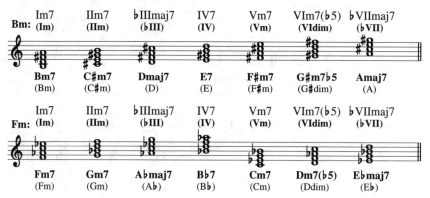

EXERCISE 17–3

Diatonic Chords in Harmonic Minor

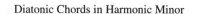

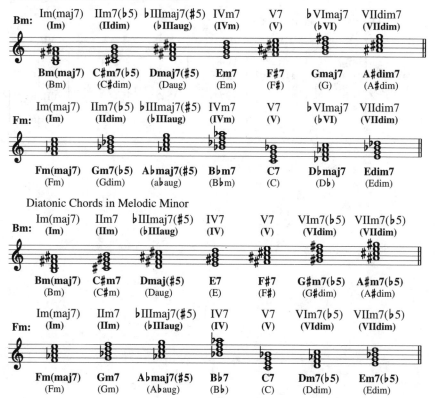

EXERCISE 17–3 (*continued*)

Diatonic Chords in Phrygian

Bm:	Im7 (Im)	$\flat$IImaj7 ($\flat$II)	$\flat$III7 ($\flat$III)	IVm7 (IVm)	Vm7($\flat$5) (Vdim)	$\flat$VImaj7 ($\flat$VI)	$\flat$VIIm7 ($\flat$VIIm)
	Bm7 (Bm)	Cmaj7 (C)	D7 (D)	Em7 (Em)	F#m7($\flat$5) (F#dim)	Gmaj7 (G)	Am7 (Am)

Fm:	Im7 (Im)	$\flat$IImaj7 ($\flat$II)	$\flat$III7 ($\flat$III)	IVm7 (IVm)	Vm7($\flat$5) (Vdim)	$\flat$VImaj7 ($\flat$VI)	$\flat$VIIm7 ($\flat$VIIm)
	Fm7 (Fm)	G$\flat$maj7 (G$\flat$)	A$\flat$7 (A$\flat$)	B$\flat$m7 (B$\flat$m)	Cm7($\flat$5) (Cdim)	D$\flat$maj7 (D$\flat$)	E$\flat$m7 (E$\flat$m)

EXERCISE 17–4

Available Diatonic Chords in Minor Key

I	II	III	IV	V	VI	VII
Im	IIm	$\flat$III	IVm	V	$\flat$VI	$\flat$VII
Im7	IIm7	$\flat$IIImaj7	IVm7	V7	$\flat$VImaj7	$\flat$VIImaj7
Im(maj7)	IIm7($\flat$5)		IV	Vm	VIm7$\flat$5	$\flat$VII7
	$\flat$II		IV7	Vm7		VIIdim7
	$\flat$IImaj7					$\flat$VIIm
						$\flat$VIIm7

EXERCISE 17–5

I Don't Wanna Cry

(T)	(SDm)	(T)	(D)		(T)	(SDM)	(T)	(D)
F#m: Im	IVm	Im	V7sus4		Im	IVm	Im	V7sus4
		M-S	M-S				M-S	M-S

$\frac{4}{4}$ F#m	Bm / F#m/A C#7sus4/G#	F#m	Bm / F#m/A C#7sus4/G#

(T)	(SDM)	(T)	(D)		(T)		(SDM)	(T)	(D)
Im	IVm	Im	V7sus4		Im		IVm	Im	V7sus4
		M-S	M-S					M-S	M-S

F#m	Bm / F#m/A C#7sus4/G#	F#m	Bm / F#m/A C#7sus4

			(D)		(D)	(D)
(SD)		(SDM)	A: V		IV/V	V
bVII		IVm	(SD)		SS	
			bVII			

E	Bm	E	D/E	E

(T)		(D)		(SD)		(D)	(D)
I		V		bVII		V7sus4 of II	V of II
		M-C					M-C

A	E/G#	G	F#7sus4	F#/A#

						(SDM)
						F#m: bVImaj7
(SD)		(T)	(SD)	(D)	(T)	(SD)	(SD)
IIm7		I	IVmaj7	V	VIm	IIm7	IVmaj7
		M-S					

Bm7 / / A/C#	Dmaj7 / E F#m	Bm7	Dmaj7

(T)	(SDM)	(T)	(D)		(T)	(SD)	(T)	(D)
Im	IVm	Im	V7sus4		Im	IVm	Im	V7sus4
			M-S				M-S	

F#m	Bm / F#m/A C#7sus4/G#	F#m	Bm / F#m/C# C#7sus4 :

			(D)		(D)		
			A: V		IV/V		
(SD)		(SDM)	(SD)		SS		(D)
bVII		IVm7	bVII				Bb:IV/V
							SS

E	Bm7	E	D/E	Eb/F

(T)		(D)		(SD)		(D)	(D)
I		V		bVII		V7sus4 of II	V of II
		M-C					M-C

Bb	F/A	Ab	G7sus4	G/B

(SD)		(T)	(SD)	(D)	(T)	(SD)	(T)	(SD)	(D)	(T)
IIm7		I	IVmaj7	V	VIm	IIm7	I	IVmaj7	V	VIm
		M-S					M-S			

Cm7 / / Bb/D	Ebmaj7 / F Gm	Cm7 / / Bb/D	Ebmaj7/ F Gm

		(SDM)		(T)		(SDM)	(T)	(D)
	Gm: bVImaj7		Im		IVm	Im	V7sus4
(SD)		(SD)					M-S	M-S
IIm7		IVmaj7						

Cm7	Ebmaj7	Gm	Cm / Gm/Bb D7sus4/A

(T)
Im

Gm

Chapter 18

EXERCISE 18–1

Tonic Minor ($\flat$III) Chords

EXERCISE 18–2

Subdominant Minor Chords

EXERCISE 18–3

How Deep Is Your Love

$E\flat$: (T) I   (T) IIIm7   (SD) IIm7   (D) V7 of II   (SD) IIm7   (D) V7 of VI   (D) IV/V

$E\flat$	Gm7	Fm7	C7	Fm7	G7	$A\flat/B\flat$

(T) I   (T) IIIm7   (T) VIm7   (SD) IIm7   (D) IV/V

$E\flat$	Gm7	Cm7	Fm7	$A\flat/B\flat$

(SD) IVmaj7   (T) IIIm7   (SD) IIm7   (SDM) $\flat$VII7

$A\flat$maj7	Gm7	Fm7	$D\flat$7

(T) IIIm7   (D) IV/V   (V9sus4)   (T) I   (T) Imaj7

Gm7	$A\flat/B\flat$	$E\flat$	$E\flat$maj7

(SD) IVmaj7   (SDM) IVm6   (T) I   (SD) $\flat$VII

$A\flat$maj7	$A\flat$m6	$E\flat$	$D\flat$

(D) V7 of II   (D) V7 of II   (SD) IIm7   (SDM) IVm6   (T) I

C7	C7	Fm7	$A\flat$m6	$E\flat$

Permissions

Baby Hold On
By Eddie Money and Jimmy Lyon
Reprinted with Permission
Copyright (c) 1978 Grajonca Music

Be My Baby Tonight
Words and Music by Ed Hill and Rich Fagan
Copyright (c) 1994 New Haven Music, Inc., Music Hill Music and OF Music
All Rights Reserved. Used by Permission.
WARNER BROS. PUBLICATIONS U.S. INC., Miami, FL. 33014

The Best of My Love
By Don Henley, Glenn Frey & John David Souther
Copyright (c) 1974 Woody Creek Music, Red Cloud Music and EMI April Music, Inc.
All rights reserved. Used by permission.
WARNER BROS. PUBLICATIONS U.S. INC., Miami, FL. 33014

Billie Jean
Written and composed by Michael Jackson
Copyright (c) 1982 Mijac Music
All Rights administered by Warner-Tamerlane Publishing Corp.
All rights reserved. Used by permission.
WARNER BROS. PUBLICATIONS U.S. INC., Miami, FL. 33014

Bridges of Love
Words and Music by Jai Josefs & Stephen Fiske
Copyright (c) Jai-Jo Music (BMI) and Fiske Music (BMI)
All Rights Reserved

Can You Read My Mind
Words by Leslie Bricusse, music by John Williams
Copyright (c) 1978 Warner-Tamerlane Publishing Corp.
All rights reserved. Used by permission.
WARNER BROS. PUBLICATIONS U.S. INC., Miami, FL. 33014

Chattahoochee
Words and Music by Jim McBride and Alan Jackson
Copyright (c) 1992 Sony Cross Keys Publishing Col, Inc., Seventh Son Music and Mattie Ruth Musick
All Rights on behalf of Sony Cross Keys Publishing Col, Inc. Administered by Sony Music Publishing, 8 Music Squre West, Nashville, TN 37209
International Copyright Secured. All Rights Reserved.

The Dance
Words and Music by Tony Arata
Copyright (c) 1989 Morganactive Songs, Inc./Pookie Bear Music (ASCAP)
All rights reserved. Used by permission.
WARNER BROS. PUBLICATIONS U.S. INC., Miami, FL. 33014

(c) 1980 ATV MUSIC CORP., MANN & WEIL SONGS, INC. Controlled and Administred by EMI BLACKWOOD MUSIC INC. under license from ATV MUSIC CORP.
All Rights Reserved. International Copyright Secured. Used by Permission.

Hey Jude
Words and Music by John Lennon and Paul McCartney
(c) 1968 NORTHERN SONGS LTD.
All Rights Controlled and Administered by EMI BLACKWOOD MUSIC INC.
under license from ATV MUSIC CORP. (MACLEN MUSIC)
All Rights Reserved. International Copyright Secured. Used by Permission.

How Am I Supposed To Live Without You
Words and Music by Michael Bolton and Doug James
(c) 1983 EMI APRIL MUSIC INC, IS HOT MUSIC and EMI BLACKWOOD MUSIC INC.
All Rights for IS NOT MUSIC Controlled and Administered by EMI APRIL MUSIC INC.
All Rights Reserved. International Copyright Secured. Used by Permission.

How Deep Is Your Love
From the Motion Picture SATURDAY NIGHT FEVER
Words and Music by Barry Gibb, Marice Gibb and Robin Gibb
Copyright (c) 1977 by Gibb Brothers Music
All Rights Administered by Careers-BMG Music Publishing, Inc.
International Copyright Secured. All Rights Reserved.

I Don't Have the Heart
Words and Music by Jud Friedman and Allan Rich
Copyright (c) 1989 Music By Candlelight, PSO Limited and Nelana Music
All rights reserved. Used by permission.
WARNER BROS. PUBLICATIONS U.S. INC., Miami, FL. 33014

I Don't Wanna Cry
Words and Music by Mariah Carey & Narada Michael Walden
Copyright (c) 1990 Gratitude Sky Music (ASCAP)/Vision Of Love Songs, Inc. (BMI)
All rights reserved. Used by permission.
WARNER BROS. PUBLICATIONS U.S. INC., Miami, FL. 33014

I Swear
Words and Music by Gary Baker and Frank Myers
Copyright (c) 1993 Rick Hall Music, Inc. & Morganactive Songs, Inc.
All rights reserved. Used by permission.
WARNER BROS. PUBLICATIONS U.S. INC., Miami, FL. 33014

I Think We're Alone Now
Written by Ritchie Cordell
Copyright (c) 1967 ABZ Music Corp. All Rights Reserved.

I Want To Know What Love Is
Words and Music by Mick Jones
Copyright (c) 1984 by Somerset Songs Publishing, Inc.
Somerset Songs Publishing, Inc. Controlled and Administered by Intersong
U.S.A., Inc.
International Copyright Secured. All Rights Reserved.

If I Ever Lose My Faith in You
Words and Music by Sting. Copyright (c) 1992 Gordon M. Sumner.
Represented by Magnetic Publishing Ltd. (PRS). Represented by Reggatta
Music Ltd. (BMI) and Administered by Irving Music Inc. (BMI) in the U.S. and
Canada.
International Copyright Secured. All Rights Reserved.

If You Asked Me To
Words and Music by Diane Warren
Copyright (c) 1989, 1990 Realsongs and UA Music Inc.
All rights reserved. Used by permission.
WARNER BROS. PUBLICATIONS U.S. INC., Miami, FL. 33014

I'll Make Love To You
Words and Music by Babyface
Copyright (c) 1994 Sony/ATV Songs, LLC and ECAF Music
All Rights Administered by Sony/ATV Music Publishing, 8 Music Square West,
Nashville, TN 37203
International Copyright Secured. All Rights Reserved.

It's Too Late
Words by Toni Stern
Music by Carole King
(c) 1971 COLGEMS-EMI MUSIC INC.
All Rights Reserved. International Copyright Secured. Used by Permission.

Jeremy
Music by Jeff Ament
Lyric by Eddie Vedder
Copyright (c) 1991 PolyGram International Publishing, Inc. Scribing C-Ment
Songs and Innocent Bystander
International Copyright Secured. All Rights Reserved.

John Deere Green
Words and Music by Dennis Linde
(c) 1993 EMI BLACKWOOD MUSIC INC. and LINDE MAJOR PUBLISHING
All Rights Controlled and Administered by EMI BLACKWOOD MUSIC INC.
All Rights Reserved. International Copyright Secured. Used by Permission.

Just Once
Words by Cynthia Weil
Music by Barry Mann

Subject Index

Song Index